STEPSON TO THE MOB

A MEMOIR OF DECISIONS, DECEPTION, AND A MOTHER'S DEEP DEVOTION

MARC BRADLEY

In loving memory of the greatest woman I have ever known. To the one who gave me life, the one who sheltered me from harm, and to the one who taught me how to laugh. This one's for you, Mom, and I hope it makes you smile.

AUTHOR'S NOTE

As I have shared random stories about my life, especially those crucial decisions that were made for me as a child, I could not begin to tell you how many times I have been told, "Bradley, you really should write a book." Now, I am certain that we all have had lives worth talking about. Maybe we've all shared with those closest to us some deep emotional events in our childhood that quite possibly changed the direction of our paths and maybe even interrupted life choices that we had hoped to have made for ourselves. I have never felt like my story was any more important or should mean any more to me than yours most certainly means to you. After all, the common denominator in all our stories has always simply been our decisions. The choices that we have made from the very beginning have brought us to where we are today.

Having said that, I must admit that in this story, the decisions that absolutely meant the most to my life were the very ones that I never got a chance to make—the ones that only those who raised me could have made.

I have decided to share my story because it was these

decisions that my mother, my biological father, and step-father made on my behalf as a young child that have been life-altering. They changed how I saw everything around me growing up. These are the kinds of memories that those around me have urged me to turn into a book.

"Yeah, maybe," I would think, followed by, "Easier said than done."

Well, I have decided that time has come. It is time to share, to the best of my ability, all the childhood memories, events, and stories that have brought me to this point in my life and inevitably to the man that I have become.

This story touches on some of the dangerous realities of the Mafia in the seventies, the witness protection program of that time, and the permanent effects that these two things had on the innocent lives of two small boys from Chicago. But one of the main focuses of this memoir is to share with you the life of a truly special woman—a woman who I am extremely proud to call my mom, a woman who was taken from us far too soon. If there is one thing I know for sure, it is that anybody who ever met this great lady has never forgotten her. With a personality that was bigger than life and a smile that could raise the roof, it is simply no surprise that my mom will forever be missed by all.

PROLOGUE

The morning started in a rush. I was in kindergarten and my brother in second grade. Mom was in more of a hurry than usual and was not her smiling, upbeat, positive self. It did not take me long to realize that my brother and I had missed the bus. Mom rushed us all into the car, all of us into the back seat, my brother, me, and our good friend Jimmy from across the street, who had missed the bus as well. There were no seatbelts back then, so the back seat was the safest place for kids our age to be. The next thing I remember is pulling out the new Partridge Family album that we had just gotten that weekend to show Jimmy. Mom had let me take it to school for show and tell, and I was really excited to show everybody. As I handed it to my friend, and just as he was turning it over to read off the songs, a Partridge Family tune from the album came over the radio. Yes, at the very moment Jimmy held the album in his hands, *I Think I Love You* started playing through the speakers. Mom realized it right away and immediately turned it up as we all started laughing and singing to the top of our lungs every word we knew. Cruising down the back road to school, passing my new album back and forth between the three of us, and singing to the Partridge Family with Mom leading the choir—now that is what growing up in the seventies was all about.

And then it happened. A moment in time that came without warning. Like an explosion of energy and speed that seemed to freeze time altogether. We had been hit. And not just hit, but literally crushed—struck with full force on Mom's side of the car by the very school bus that we had missed that morning. All I know is the initial impact and the sound that it made has never really left me. The car rolled halfway onto its side and then spun around until it finally landed in an empty field. I ended up across the other side of the car on the floorboard as my brother flew up into the front seat under the dashboard.

As I came to, I realized what had just happened. I noticed that Jimmy was still in the same place in the back seat and still holding the vinyl record, out of its sleeve, and still in perfect condition. I immediately looked up to the driver's seat to see if Mom was OK. It was all a blur, but my mom was obviously frantic in the moment. She was all about making sure we were OK as she continued to cover her nose with her hand. I could not tell what had exactly happened to her, but I remember the blood. There was blood all over the steering wheel and blood on her hands and face. Police officers surrounded the car, and I heard ambulance sirens all around us. At some point, we were taken from the car and split up for medical attention.

The next thing I knew, I was sitting on the floor in the downstairs den of my friend Jimmy's house. Jimmy, my brother, and I were playing a game of some sort as Jimmy's mom, Danna, was fixing lunch off in the kitchen.

She had the radio on in the background and turned it up when the great Neil Diamond's classic, *Cracklin' Rosie,* came on. That iconic voice sang those memorable lyrics in a moment of complete fear and stress on my young mind and heart. To this day, that song will always bring me back to that event, as do many great songs of my childhood. They've become the markers to my life's story and many of the events in it.

We were all worried about Mom, and nothing else seemed to matter. Danna had just told us that she had suffered a broken nose and would need emergency surgery. I could really sense the seriousness in Danna's voice as she kept us informed throughout the day. Danna was Mom's absolute best friend and someone that my brother and I trusted and loved very much. I always felt a sense of true happiness and comfort whenever we spent time at their house. We had to stay overnight a night or two until Mom was able to come home from the hospital.

What was most important to me, at the age of five, was not really the crash itself, but the fact that Mom needed emergency nose surgery after breaking it against the steering wheel of the car. It was during that operation that the unthinkable happened. While under extreme pressure to give her the blood transfusion that she needed, as things were obviously happening very quickly, she contracted hepatitis C. This was not something you ever wanted to get, especially back in the seventies, when they knew far less how to treat this disease than we do now. This was kept from us, though, and it would be many years before we would learn the truth of that devastating disease.

1

BORN FOR BEAUTY SCHOOL

I was born Bradley Mark Morrow on July 11, 1966, and grew up in the suburban Chicago town of Hazel Crest until I was seven years old. All the houses were that extremely popular split-level build, and ours seemed no different from anybody else's on the block, except the color. It was a gray-black with banana yellow window shutters and a matching yellow door—something that you just could not miss. I remember when it was painted and the reaction all the neighbors had. There is no doubt that this was Mom's way of standing out and away from that very boring, traditional neighborhood look of the '60s and '70s. If there was one thing my mom was not, it was boring. Not even close. She was the absolute life of the party and the one who just lit up a room as soon as she walked into it.

She was born Vivien Lee McDade on May 15, 1945, the daughter of Archie and Virginia and sibling to her younger brother, Robert. One truth that always saddened me about her childhood was the fact that her mother, Virginia, was extremely strict and often very mean to her.

Strict punishments and lots of verbal abuse took their toll on her as a child and caused her to escape from it all to my nana's house as often as she possibly could.

Nana—Mom's grandmother and Virginia's mother—was just a hoot of a woman. She was so loving, kind, and incredibly funny. I know now where the great sense of humor came from in the family. Mom certainly had it, and I am proud to say that I was blessed to catch that humor bug myself. It certainly made perfect sense why Mom insisted on spending all the time she could with Nana. However, as mean and abusive as Grandma McDade was to her only daughter, she was just the opposite to her only son, my Uncle Bobby. Grandma McDade always treated Bobby with kid gloves. He was the baby by seven years to mom and could do no wrong in her eyes. And, to make matters worse, she often boasted about what a great child he was. Grandma inflicted constant abuse toward my mom and nothing but love and attention to little Bobby.

Other than my mother's escapes to Nana's every chance she got, her other saving grace was living in the very same home with her. It was her loving father, Archie. Grandpa McDade was her absolute hero. In fact, I am convinced that he and Nana are the reasons she emotionally survived through all that pain and suffering handed out by her mother all those years. He came to her defense from Virginia's wrath as often as he possibly could, but he too was afraid of her and clearly did not, as they say, "wear the pants in the family."

Mom soon began rebelling as she hit the teenage years, and it was not long before things reached a tipping point in the McDade home. Mom became pregnant at the age of fifteen, and, as much as that is very much frowned upon in today's world, back in 1960, it was considered the ultimate sin. It was simply catastrophic, to say the least. Not knowing what to do, she turned to the one she trusted the most in her life: her dad. If anybody could help her understand this, love and comfort her through it, and never condemn her for it, it was Archie. Of course, once Grandma McDade found out, she did not make it easy on anybody. She kicked Mom out of the house and wanted nothing to do with her.

Fortunately, Mom was welcomed at Nana's house and stayed there throughout the pregnancy. The decision was made that she would give up the baby for adoption once it was born and, in doing so, would allow a newborn baby boy a real chance at the best life possible. I did not hear of this story until much later into my adult life and have always wondered about that half brother of mine. Is he out there somewhere, living his life happy and content? Maybe married, maybe with beautiful children? Would he look like Mom? Did he get that great sense of humor? If we ever met, would he want to hear everything about her? I may never know the answer to these questions, but I do know one thing. If it is God's will that we meet someday, then surely it will happen.

Though one might think becoming pregnant at fifteen, then giving the baby up for adoption, would be the worst of the teenage adolescent drama; unfortunately, it was not. After all of that, Mom decided that going back to school was not something she wanted to do. What she really wanted was to become a hairdresser and had decided that going to beauty school was her only way of achieving that. Everybody around her knew how much she loved to do hair, especially her girlfriends, who insisted she always be the one to style up their hairdos at all the sleepovers. However, she did not want to wait until finishing high school to do so, and that was the big problem. When her mother learned of this, she was beside herself with anger, and things got very heated very fast. Grandma McDade was a schoolteacher and obviously believed that education was paramount. She refused to accept her daughter dropping out of high school, especially to become a beautician.

So, once again, Grandma McDade wanted nothing to do with her and again wanted her out of the house. Mom again turned to the only one in the household that had always supported her with love and understanding: her dad. He did understand her love for the world of hairstyling very much and always knew that someday she would become a great stylist. But he also understood the importance of a good education. So, they compromised and came up with a plan. Mom would enroll in beauty school, graduate, and then immediately return to high school to finish up and receive her diploma. That decision also helped keep her mother happy enough to at least allow her to continue living at home. So, it was done. Mom completed beauty school, got certified, and then went back and finished high school.

The next event to take place that had the McDade residents up in arms came when Mom met and began dating a man who would eventually become my biological father. To say the least, Grandma McDade hated this man. She did not want Mom seeing him and made it clear that if the relationship continued, then she would no longer be allowed to live at home. Mom was young, barely out of school, and at least for the moment, thought she was in love. Archie tried to keep the peace but, in the end, to no avail. Mom refused to stop seeing him and was inevitably kicked out.

2

COOL CARS

Not long after my mother moved in with my biological father, she became pregnant. And soon after, because it seemed like the right thing to do, they got married. By the time Mom was nineteen, she had given birth to my brother, and I was born just two short years later. She was twenty-one years old and married to a man just a couple of years older than her. It was 1966 in Chicago, and there were now two little boys to raise. Her family was supportive in the beginning except for one: her mother. Grandma McDade, unfortunately, had not spoken to her daughter since mom was kicked out of their home and had not yet even seen her young grandchildren.

It was not long after I was born that this marriage, which seemed to be based more on a pregnancy than real love, began to disintegrate. Alcohol, infidelity, verbal abuse, and immaturity lead to a divorce, and Grandma McDade must have welcomed this event with open arms.

I have no recollection of ever living with my biological father while they were married. However, the first memories I have as a child all took place while living in the split-level home in Hazel Crest, which always led me to believe that Mom and my biological father were the first to live there. That home is where I slowly discovered the reality that there had been a divorce. Not that I knew what a divorce even was, but I understood that there were now two men involved with my life. There was my biological father, who would pick us up every other Saturday to spend the night with him and his girlfriend at their apartment. And then there was a man named Al, who lived in our home. Al, as the story goes, swept my mother off her feet at a time when her marriage to my father was failing. And because he, too, was in a failing marriage of his own, it would be just a matter of time before these two would fall in love, leave their spouses, and begin living their lives together.

One Saturday, my brother and I had to decide who we wanted to go with during my dad's visitation: our father or Al. It was the first time we had to make this kind of choice. Before this, our father picked us up every other Saturday, took us to his apartment for the night, and brought us home the next day. That was it. But this day was different. On this Saturday morning, Mom had us in the kitchen, where she began to explain how it might be possible that, if one of us wanted to go with Al for the day, and the other with our father, then that would be OK. I sat, very confused, on the kitchen counter as my brother adamantly stated that he had no interest in spending time with Al and was going with our dad. I noticed my mom's sad expression at my brother's reaction, and I felt sorry for her and bad for Al. Just the thought of mom being unhappy hurt me, and because I could not let that happen, I jumped off the counter and said "yes," agreeing to go with Al for the day in hopes that it would satisfy everybody.

That same day, I sat on another counter—this one in an auto garage where I was eating a great burger and fries while watching Al hard at work taking apart bumpers from cars, removing engines, and even painting some as well. I thought the colors were cool on those cars. There were a whole bunch of men in this shop working away, and Al seemed to really enjoy having me there as he introduced me to as many of them as he could. I, too, enjoyed the experience very much. I began to take a real liking to this new man in our lives.

That day I spent at that auto shop would not be my last, as Mom would continue to give us the choice of who we wanted to spend those Saturdays with. I often chose the time with Al, eating those great burgers for lunch and watching all those cool cars get painted. My brother never did. He always chose the time to spend with our father. He did not seem to have much, if any, interest in what it was Al did or did not do for a living. He was two years older and had a closer connection to our father and certainly a better understanding of who Al was in our lives. To him, Al was the new guy there to replace his father, and he was having no part of it.

My mom and Al threw parties for all their friends and neighbors. I always knew when they were going to have one as they would send us to bed earlier than usual, allow for some time to go by, and then, in hopes that we were fast asleep, let the music play. It would start at a low volume, just enough for us to hear who it was. Often, Mom started the night with Sly and the Family Stone or the James Gang; other nights, it might be James Taylor or Carole King. But one thing was for sure: by the end of the night, it was all Joe Cocker. From *Delta Lady* to *Dear Landlord*, from *High Time We Went* to *Space Captain*, she had it all, and we grew up listening to it all. Even if we, at times, would doze off during the party, we always managed to wake up when the Cocker tunes came on, and we heard the sound of Mom's enthusiastic cheers and laughter. Her one-of-a-kind energy carried the party on through the night with singing and dancing. And, yes, there was plenty of alcohol. Booze was as much a part of it as the music itself. And I am sure for some guests, more than just that. After all, it was the late sixties, early seventies, and at least from what I could see around me, it was simply a part of life.

Sometimes, as the party was in full swing, I would sneak out of bed and crawl to the crack in my door and push it open just enough to get a glimpse of what was happening. Rarely could I see much down the hallway, but it always made me feel like I was part of the action, and that was so exciting to me. I had a real connection to that energy. Listening to how much fun Mom was having and all the hooting and hollering going on from everybody there, I wanted so badly to be a part of it and to be the life of the party too. I wanted to help Mom choose the music and dance right alongside her. Witnessing how much fun and excitement that it brought to people would have a huge and lasting impression on me.

Everybody simply called my mom "Viv," and she was as "one of a kind" as it got. Her smile and energy captivated everyone around her. All the neighbors around Hazel Crest came to visit our home quite often for a couple of good reasons: they loved her company, and they came to get their hair done. Mom had become a licensed beautician and had set up her own salon in the basement of our home. It was down there that a lot of the wild and crazy events took place. I would hang out with all the "shampoo set ladies" while Mom did their hair. In these days before school, I was home with her all day, every day, and would spin around in the chairs while the great music of the time would play from our classic counsel stereo set. Whether it was Janis Joplin or the Spinners, it put all the ladies in a great mood. Sometimes Mom would even let me play them my Partridge Family records, as they would watch me dance and lip-sync every word I knew.

It was clear that my need to be the life of the party, just like her, was beginning at an incredibly young age.

One morning, I decided to go down and show the shampoo set ladies my new cowboy gun and holster set. I walked around to all the beauty chairs, with my cool holster set strapped around my waist like a real cowboy, pulling out my pistols occasionally and telling them to put their hands up. The ladies laughed hysterically as I put on my show. But what I had not realized was that I was in such a hurry to strap on my holster and gun set, I forgot to put on any clothes. I mean, not a stitch. And even though Mom was laughing right along with everybody, she finally had to stop her little streaker from holding up any more of her customers until she could get him to put some clothes on.

3

ROLLER SKATES AND ROCK 'N' ROLL

As my early years continued as a small boy in Hazel Crest, my brother and I finally did get the opportunity to spend time at Grandma McDade's house. At some point after Mom's divorce from my father, she and her mom had made amends, and that finally allowed relationships to be built with all involved. We both gleamed with excitement anytime Mom would announce we were headed over to see the family and especially to hang out with Uncle Bob. At this point, he had graduated from high school and was heading to college at Drake University. He was to study geology as he had a real passion for the study of rocks. He was also a real athlete in track and had received a scholarship for both academics and track and field. Bob even shared with us a true love of music. As Mom's favorites were the likes of Janis Joplin, Sly and the Family Stone and, most of all, Joe Cocker, Bob's were of a real depth musically like Chick Correa, Santana, and Emerson, Lake & Palmer.

My brother and I would rush down to the basement as soon as we walked in the door to find him listening to all that great music through his giant headphones. As soon as he saw us, he would pull off the headset and turn up the tunes for us to enjoy with him. But that was just the beginning of the fun. Uncle Bob was not just a young, smart, attractive, athletic, and fun-loving guy, he was also an exceptionally good drummer. And sitting in the corner of that basement was a big, beautiful drum set that he just loved to play for us. We would sit around the set for hours while he played along to those great songs spinning on the phonograph. There is just no doubt the love of music that was shared by everyone around me—whether it was Mom hosting her parties, cranking up the radio in the car, or watching my uncle play drums in the basement—played an instrumental role in who I became.

One afternoon, my brother and I were roller skating in the driveway in front of Grandma's house when this music came blaring from the house across the cul-de-sac. It was definitely not from a record and was clearly coming from musicians playing live. But what really confused us was the fact that we couldn't see anybody. The garage was shut, and though there were many cars parked around the house, there was no evidence of actual people playing music. Mom was out there with us too and had no idea what exactly was going on. Grandma soon came walking outside toward the thunder of power chords, shaking her head in disappointment.

"Oh my goodness, not again!" she said. "How many times are we going to have to put up with this?"

Clearly unhappy, she went on to explain that this was a routine band practice for her neighbor's teenage son and his bandmates. She told us that all the neighbors had complained, but the young man's parents continued to let them jam. They always stuck up for their son and his bandmates and would let them play for as long as they wanted up until it got dark. Grandma McDade was friends with the boy's mother, so that made it hard for her to complain too much about it, and she would never show her frustration directly to Mrs. Cronin. They had been living as neighbors in that suburb of Oak Lawn for many years, and even though Grandma was not a very sociable woman, she was quite close to Mille. It seemed that almost every time we visited Grandma's house, at some point in the day, that band would start up and rock the cul-de-sac away. My brother and I would just stand in the driveway, our little bodies vibrating to the melody of the electric guitars and that solid thump of the bass drum. We were mesmerized and couldn't take our eyes or ears away from it. I cannot say that I ever really knew what was being played, but it was just exciting to be a part of it. Some days, they would have the garage open, which was really cool, even though it was almost impossible to make out what any of them looked like. There was just lots of hair and plenty of rock and roll!

In the midst of all of that long hair shaking and loud music blasting was a voice. And that voice my brother and I would always hear was coming from none other than Mrs. Cronin's son. Grandma, like the rest of Mrs. Cronin's friends, just called her Mille and the son they called Kevin—as in the late Mildred "Mille" Cronin and the rock icon Kevin Cronin, lead singer for the legendary rock band REO Speedwagon! That garage was the place where it all began for him. And I have always thought how awesome it was that Kevin's parents, no matter how much the neighborhood complained of that dreaded rock 'n' roll noise, never stopped supporting their son.

4

THE TIDE BEGINS TO TURN

It was a typical Sunday morning, with our father dropping my brother and me off after a night at his apartment. We walked in the house ready to greet Mom at the door, only to be met by our nana. This was not normal as we usually only saw her when we visited her house. We immediately asked where Mom was, and Nana responded sadly that she and Al had not made it home from their previous night out but should return soon. Even though I was only six years old, I knew down deep that something wasn't right. There was something about the way Nana answered us, the sound of her voice and her expression, that said it all.

I cried for Mom to come home as Nana tried to settle us in with comforting words that everything was fine and not to worry.

What seemed like hours later, Mom and Al finally came through the front door. Her amazing smile lit up the room when she saw us as I ran to her for one of those big warm hugs. Finally, Mom was home, and everything seemed to be OK. She looked at us with both empathy and excitement in her eyes.

"Boys, I am so sorry I had the two of you worried, but when you hear where we went, I'm sure you will understand," she said. Her smile grew again as she announced, "We went to see Joe Cocker in concert last night and wait till I tell you what happened!"

We shared her excitement as we begged her to tell us everything.

Mom began with a sadness in her voice, telling us that Joe had disappointed everyone by never making it to the stage at all.

"He just never came to the stage," she explained. "After we waited through an extended intermission that seemed like forever and as the crowd became more agitated, Joe failed to make it."

"When the lights did finally go out for showtime, I anxiously watched for him to come out. I looked from side to side when the glare of a flashlight caught my eye, and that's when I saw it. They were lighting the steps for him to walk up when he stumbled and fell onto the edge of the stage. His security held him as he began to vomit all over the stairs. The crowd saw this, and though at first paused in shock, they soon began to boo loudly as the crew picked him up and rushed him backstage."

Mom seemed on the brink of tears as she went on to explain that it took even longer for them to inevitably announce the show was canceled.

Because it was so late, she said, they decided to stay overnight and drive back in the morning.

My brother and I couldn't believe what we were hearing, and I felt so bad for Mom, knowing how devastated she must have been. Her absolute favorite artist of all time, and finally, with an opportunity to see him in concert, this happens. We couldn't help but ask why he was so sick.

"They said he had, unfortunately, drank too much wine before the show and was simply too drunk to perform," she replied as she wiped her tears.

Though this seemed to be the conclusion to a sad story, Mom immediately switched gears and, with that glow back on her face, began to tell us all about how great Ike and Tina Turner were, who had evidently opened for him. She described how Tina had on this wild fishnet dress and just danced and sang like no other. Mom could never just tell the story without adding in all of the action that went with it, so without hesitation, she went into her "Tina dance!"

"Woot," she cried, "Bradley, go grab their 8-track, the one with *Proud Mary*, and let me show you how she did it!"

I raced down to the basement and grabbed the tape along with some much-needed Joe Cocker as a way of helping to heal her heart. Into the 8-track player it went, and for the next couple of hours, we danced and sang like crazy! Mom gave us her best Tina moves as my brother, and I did our best to keep up with her during the fast part of Ike and Tina's legendary version of CCR's classic *Proud Mary*.

The night wasn't complete, however, until we threw on Joe Cocker's second album and cranked up songs like *Lawdy Miss Clawdy* and *Feelin' Alright* along with his amazing cover of the Beatles' *She Came in Through the Bathroom Window*! To hear Mom's hoots and hollers while we all danced up a storm was all I needed to confirm in my heart that everything was back to normal.

That day would come and go, but there would still be another day when we came home from our fathers to see

Nana, and not our mother, greeting us at the door. Only this time, Mom and Al would be absent even longer. This hiatus would go on for two straight days, leaving Nana to split the duties of watching us between her and Mom's best friend Danna. This time it would not be as easy to explain to us where these two were, and it was evident there was trouble. Danna explained that they had gone out of town to see a music festival and would be home very soon. Not knowing what a music festival was, I certainly could not understand this. But we trusted Danna very much and got to sleep over at her house and play with our good friend Jimmy, so we made the best of it.

Once Mom returned home, everything seemed to go back to normal again. But this new kind of normal just did not feel right. Things were changing, and even as a young boy who was easily distracted, I sensed the stress around me. There was also something else going on that, though at the time seemed quite exciting to me, was very unusual. We seemed to constantly have exceedingly rare and awfully expensive automobiles showing up at the house. All types of them, too, from a classic green 1923 Model-T Ford to a custom cocoa brown '57 T-Bird complete with a convertible hardtop and black button tuck leather interior.

One day, a beautiful hot orange '68 Camaro pulled up, and this seemed to be more than just a cool car pulling up in the driveway. Mom saw it and just went crazy! She ran down the steps of the porch, screaming, "Is this for me, Al? Oh, please tell me it's for me!"

Al stepped out of that beauty with the keys held up and said, "Yes it is, babe," as he dropped them in her hand. She screamed for joy while she hugged him as my brother and I looked on. It was an exciting moment, and I was so happy for Mom. But I could not escape an uneasy feeling that this wasn't normal at all.

Besides the new Camaro for Mom and a couple of custom-painted Harley-Davidson Sportsters, most of these pristine collectors would come and go, staying just long enough for everybody to enjoy them and then disappear as if it never happened.

If there was one thing that all these events had in common, it was that this new man of the house named Al was connected to them. All these vehicles, after all, were being brought to the house, driven by him, and presented to us as gifts. Mom always told us that these were just some of the cars that Al worked on and built at that body shop he often took me to. It made sense, I suppose, considering that is what they told us he did for a living. And how were boys our age to know any better?

Our nana greeted us at the door on two different occasions on our return home from our father's, when up until then, it had always been Mom. Without exception, she was always the one to greet us whether returning from our father's or our friend's, or even from school. After all, she worked from home in her beauty shop downstairs, and that certainly in itself was a big reason why I felt so close to her and so loved being around her twenty-four seven.

If there is one thing for sure, the music always played around us, and I mean ALWAYS! Coming into the house with the sounds of Joe Cocker or Janis Joplin blasting through the stereo while she was either running the vacuum or busy with a client in the basement was a normal occurrence. So, when things were not that way, and she was nowhere to be found, it stood to reason why these two little boys would have questions. And though we were indeed given answers, things just didn't seem to add up.

I suppose the reason for being absent the first time with the Joe Cocker concert made sense and seemed truthful. After all, Mom had told us all about how great Ike and Tina were and how disappointed she was about having to miss Joe. But then there was the weekend music festival—the one that caused them to be gone for over two days due to a rainstorm. At this time, it was 1972-'73, and though their description sounded an awful lot like Woodstock, that festival had taken place in 1969.

And in the midst of all of this, Al seemed to have nonstop access to very expensive and very rare toys. It was all these very peculiar events, along with a whole lot more going on in secret than one could ever imagine, that would begin to ultimately shape our exit from Chicago. It would be a departure from our family, our friends, our neighbors. Just like that. One day we were there, and the next, we were not. But how could this be? What about Nana, Uncle Bob, Grandma McDade, or our father? All our neighbor friends, classmates, aunts, and cousins? Not to mention all of mom's beauty-shop clientele. They would all be left behind, and only the four of us would depart from Southside Hazel Crest. But why? And for how long? And why so quickly? Only time would tell us these things, and by this point, time began moving very swiftly.

5

WHERE ARE WE?

In 1973, when I was seven years old, I was awoken out of a deep sleep to the sound of my mom's soft voice telling my nine-year-old brother to wake up. I looked toward his bed and could barely see the silhouette of my mom, sitting on the edge, moving his shoulders to get his attention. He finally started to move to his feet. My sleepy mind didn't understand anything that was going on and wondered if she was only waking him or whether I would be next. Moments later, that question was answered as she had me get up as well and then asked us both to put some clothes on over our pajamas.

We were confused, asking why we had to get up and get dressed, but all she would say was, "Come on, boys. I don't have time to explain now, but I will. We just have to go. It's time to go." With a gentle tone, she continued, "You two will soon be able to go back to sleep, and that's why you can leave your PJs on for now."

"But Mom, why do we have to leave?" I asked. "And where do we have to go?"

She kneeled down in front of me, held my two hands,

and replied, "Bradley Mark, the three of us have to go for a little drive, but don't you worry, because before you know it, you'll be back to sleep and once you wake again I will tell you all about what's going on."

She squeezed my little hands tighter and said, "But for now, we have to hurry. Al is waiting on us."

I nodded in agreement and continued trying to find my clothes.

The only source of light came from the hall bathroom, which made it very difficult to see enough to find anything. My brother reached to turn on the bedroom light, and Mom stopped him right away.

"No, no, we need to keep the lights off, boys. Don't worry; I'm right here to help you find your things."

As strange as this all was for us, and as confusing as it all seemed, I felt calm and willing to do whatever she asked. Just the fact that she spoke with such a loving voice and seemed to know exactly what was happening made me feel secure. Mom just had a way of always making us feel safe no matter what was going on.

Half asleep, we walked down the hall to the opening of the staircase, lit by a flashlight pointed toward the ground as we approached. Who was holding the flashlight was unknown. As my eyes got clearer, I did not recognize anyone around me. Down the stairs we went, my brother taking the lead as I made a point to stay as close to Mom as I possibly could. As that flashlight followed our every step toward the landing, I was startled by a strange man who stood at the bottom. He said nothing as he opened the door for us, but once outside, he looked at Mom and said, "Viv, you three will be with Al in that black Lincoln over there." He pointed in the direction of the car sitting in front of the house, still running with the headlights on.

The sight of those headlights would remain burned in my memory forever.

My eyes followed the man's finger directly to the long black Continental awaiting us. It was so dark outside that if not for those beaming headlights, I certainly would have never seen it. The man on the porch, using his flashlight, led us down the stairs and across the driveway to the vehicle. He opened the back door, and immediately the dome light came on. There, I saw another man I did not recognize sitting in the driver's seat, and next to him sat Al. My brother crawled in first, followed by Mom and then me. The man shut the door behind us, and immediately the inside of the car went dark. It was at that moment that I lost it. I was now frightened and suddenly did not feel safe at all. What was happening to us, and who were these strange men around us? Why are we leaving our home and especially at this time of night? And, most importantly, where are we going?

"No, Mom, please!" I cried out. "I don't want to go; I don't want to leave!"

She immediately had the driver turn the dome light back on as she held me in her arms.

"Shh," she whispered. "Bradley, come here," She squeezed tighter. "Everything's going to be OK. I'm right here, and nothing is going to happen to you two."

She continued to hold me as I wept in her arms. Her soothing words slowly calmed me, and before long, I settled into her lap. The dome light turned to black, and we pulled away. But where exactly were we headed, and why? As I dozed off, I kept hearing the words "airport" and "airplane" mentioned, but my brother and I slept through most all the drive.

When I awoke, it was still dark as Mom led us out of the car and into a large building with long glass sliding doors. Surrounded by lots of hustle and bustle, and many people with suitcases, it was clear we were in an airport and soon to board an airplane. The next thing I knew, we were thirty thousand feet in the air, and I was extremely airsick. As a first-time flier, I was not doing well at all. I held that airline bag in one hand and Mom's hand in the other the entire flight.

We landed, and things then began to happen very quickly. We checked into a hotel, where my brother and I were immediately asked to go out into the hallway and play. We both laid on the floor playing with the toy cars Mom had brought for us as a strange man standing next to the door watched on. He was very tall, dressed in a suit and tie and wearing a long khaki trench coat. He seemed very interested in what my brother and I were up to and even offered to join in the fun as we pushed our cars across the hall. I asked him who he was and, with a smile and an inviting handshake, he said, "Why, my name is Schmitty, and what is yours, young man?"

I cautiously held out my hand and answered, "Bradley, and I'm seven."

Schmitty chuckled at that and replied, "Well, it's very nice to meet you, Bradley, and, just so you know, I'm here to keep you two boys company, so I hope that's OK?"

We both said, "Sure," and with that, the fun began.

Schmitty was a very funny man, and we really enjoyed our time in the hall with him. There was also one thing that was quite evident about our newfound friend, despite having fun with us: he was certainly keeping watch. And not just over us, but over everything. In fact, most of the time, there were two men, one on either side of the door, standing upright and looking extremely focused. As we continued playing outside the room, at one point, I looked up at Schmitty and asked, "How come we have to play out here and not in the room with Mom?"

"Oh, don't worry, Bradley," he replied, "Your mom is just talking over some things with Al, and once they're done, you guys can go back in; I promise."

I smiled and immediately felt confident we were in good hands with these two men in suits. Sure enough, Mom did let us back into the room, and all the men who were in there talking with her and Al finally left.

This would go on for two days, with my brother and me going back and forth from the room to the hallway as Schmitty and his partner would continue keeping a watchful eye over us and do their best to keep us entertained. We became quite fond of this funny man in the trench coat. He would eventually become someone especially important in our lives. There was, however, a lot we just did not yet know.

6

TOPEKA, KANSAS?

Here we are, just a few months after arriving in our
new town.

Our seventy-two-hour journey would finally come to an end, landing us in the chosen destination—a small city called Topeka in the state of Kansas. In what seemed like the blink of an eye, we went from two small boys growing up in the Windy City of Chicago to two very confused boys walking into an empty apartment in a capital city that most had never heard of. We were located just south of the Capitol Building in an apartment complex called Carriage House and would seemingly settle in as any normal family would. A select few of those strange men that had been with us throughout this move would continue their presence in assisting with anything we needed. None would be more helpful than our favorite new friend, Schmitty, who always seemed to be around to make us feel comfortable in this strange new life. Though acclimating to all of this certainly took time, my brother and I eventually fell right into the swing of things. Establishing our surroundings and getting ready to start in a new school became part of the excitement.

One evening, after dinner and just a few days before we were to start school, mom and Al sat us down for a family talk. We all sat at our octagon-shaped dining room table as my brother and I spun around in the faux leather green swivel chairs, uncertain what this was all about. They began by explaining that the new kids and teachers we would meet in our new school were going to naturally ask us where we were from.

"And we tell them we are from Chicago, right?" I quickly asked.

"Well, yes, that is what you tell them, Bradley," my mom said. "But if they ask why you moved here, you two will need to know what to say."

She looked at Al as she spoke those words as if to turn the conversation over to him. Without hesitation, he continued Mom's point.

"I know you boys have had a lot of questions about why we moved here," Al said, "and your mom and I think it is time that you understand more about what really happened."

Those words immediately stopped me from swiveling in my chair as I now locked into every word.

"You see, all these men who have been around us," he continued, "are called US Marshals and have all been assigned to help protect us during this move."

Though he was making eye contact with both of us, he also kept looking over at Mom as if to get her assurance that he was saying everything correctly, almost as if it were rehearsed. I looked at both of them as Al continued, wondering whether any of this made any real sense. I jumped in with the obvious question. "Why do we need them to protect us? What did we do?"

"No, no," Al replied, "it's nothing we did; it is something that someone else actually did to me. The truth is, I am also a US federal marshal, and I work with all these men."

My eyes grew bigger, and my heart began beating faster.

"That body shop I took you to, Bradley, was indeed where I worked, but not as a body shop attendant," he explained. "I was working as a marshal under cover to arrest a man who was a well-known car thief, and because he had become a friend of mine during the process, he did not take this arrest well."

Al went on to tell us that this man had made serious threats on his life, and it was necessary that we take all possible precautions to keep ourselves safe.

"We are all now part of what they call a witness protection program," he said. "It's a way to keep us safe from anything this man might try to do."

"And these men Al works with thought that the further away we get from his friend, the less chance he has of ever finding us," Mom added.

"So, I don't want either of you to worry about anything because everything is going to be just fine, and we are all very safe here."

Al followed up with more assurance that his friend was actually very afraid of him and would never be foolish enough to pursue any of the threats he had made. He said it with a real tough-guy type confidence, almost cocky as he explained with a smile.

"Now, it is very important that if you boys are ever asked why you moved here all the way from Chicago that you tell them this," he continued. "You tell them your stepfather had to transfer with his job, and this is where they chose to send him."

He then insisted that we never speak of the friend who threatened him and never include that part of the story.

My brother and I sat silent as we tried our best to process all of this. Mom looked at us both with love and compassion in her eyes and said, "And I don't want you two to ever forget, we are all very safe here, and we have a lot to be excited about! New school, new friends, and a whole new town to do it in!"

Her excitement was actually believable, and it certainly helped put a smile on my face, but something still didn't feel right. It was obvious that we needed to know what the circumstances were that brought us from our two-story home in Hazel Crest to this small apartment in Topeka, and it seemed they had accomplished that for us. However, it just didn't seem possible that an incident like Al had described could have caused such drastic recourse.

I sat at the table, looking at this man across from me, who I knew my mom loved but who I no longer knew at all. I would never again, from that day forward, see this man in the same light.

The four of us would continue settling in as smoothly as possible, considering the incredible circumstances. However, it wasn't long before a surprise would show up at our front door. One day after my brother and I got home from school, Mom greeted us at the door just bubbling over with excitement.

"You two are not going to believe what's happening today when Al gets back home," she said. "Something's arriving from Chicago that I have been waiting on for a long time now!" Neither one of us could hold back our curiosity as we both shouted, "What, Mom; what is it?!"

Just as she was about to answer, we heard a car honking loudly outside the apartment, and we immediately ran out to see what it was all about. As we turned the corner of the building and put our eyes on the parking lot, there it was: that beautiful hot orange '68 Camaro that Al had given Mom back in Chicago, complete with classic Cragar mag rims gleaming with blinding sparkle and the black rag top rolled back. Mom exploded with excitement at the sight of that beauty.

"Oh my goodness, Al; you got it back!" she screamed, "You finally got it back for me!"

He stood outside that hotrod with the door open while the thunderous motor idled, holding out those keys again for her to take. She grabbed them up and said, "Come on, boys, we're going for a drive!" Without hesitation, my brother and I jumped in, and off we went. I sat shotgun, with my brother in the back, as Mom floored it out of the apartment complex. My head kept jolting back with every push of the gas pedal as the radio blasted the classic Steve Miller tune, The Joker. We were definitely the envy on the streets that day, there was no doubt.

Yet, as time went on, more vehicles would show up, including a long white Lincoln Continental Mark III, which became Al's everyday driver. According to Mom, all our belongings would gradually show up from Chicago as her best friend, Danna, was put in charge of getting everything together. Evidently, Mom had confided in her from the start, and Danna had agreed to help in any way that we needed her to. Sadly, however, there would be a phone call made from Danna to Mom that would inform her of some bad news. It seemed that our house had been vandalized at some point during this operation and was essentially whipped out. Many things were stolen, including the two Harley-Davidson choppers from the garage, and much was also destroyed. So, needless to say, we went without much furniture during the early days of our apartment life.

The United States Marshals Service had evidently established a plan in which we would spend the first six months in the location at Carriage House and then move on to another apartment complex just down the street, where we would then spend another year. Mom and Al sat us both down again one afternoon to explain all of this. They said it would act as a way of keeping the relocation process undetected while we continued to establish normalcy. During this family discussion, however, that wasn't the only thing we would learn. We would discover there were more changes involved than just an address or two.

"We need you both to understand something about our names," Mom said, "and I don't mean either of your names. You will always be who you are and always keep the names that you two have. I am talking about my name and Al's as well. Our last names are no longer what they were when we got married and were changed as soon as we committed to relocating."

She stated their new last names to us and then, with a serious emphasis in her tone, said, "Now, I want you boys to always remember what our new names are and make sure that if anyone ever asked, that you know exactly what to tell them."

We agreed as I drew a real sense of relief that the only change in Mom's name was her last. Although she was always just "Mom" to me, I always loved her name and when people called her "Viv."

As 1973 rolled into '74, and we had moved from one apartment to the next, Mom was now working for a local beauty salon, where she began to build quite a clientele. Of all the qualities she possessed, being an outstanding hairdresser was certainly at the top of the list. Al, on the other hand, did something that we could have never expected. Despite having been transferred with the Marshals Service, strangely, he did not continue working as one. Instead, he bought a gas station just down the street from our apartment, equipped with a full-service automotive repair shop, and even joined up with a business partner. So, just like that and out of the blue, Al became a full-time owner/mechanic of a Skelly gas station and began what would seem to be his newfound career.

When 1975 came, and it was time to move again, Mom explained to us in a little more detail how these decisions about where to live were being made. Evidently, it was during the time we had spent at the hotels on our way to Kansas that most of these discussions took place. While my brother and I were playing in the hallways with Schmitty, they discussed what the next moves would be.

"The marshals had asked me where we would eventually like to live," she said, then smiled and declared, "and I immediately told them Florida."

Her smile faded a bit as she added, "But they said it was still too early for a move like that, but assured me when the time was right, they would make it happen for us."

That is when she said they first mentioned the name Topeka to both of them, and with a laugh, she admitted she wasn't even sure how to spell it, let alone knew where it was. They explained to her that was exactly the idea. They sent us first to a town that would go undetected by anyone who could be looking for Al. It would be a safe, temporary hiding place until enough time had gone by that the Marshals Service felt confident things were safe and secure for a more permanent move. Mom told us she also asked about immediate family. When would they be allowed to contact loved ones back home to let them know what was going on and, inevitably, when they could see them again?

Though Mom would explain that the marshals gave no guarantee of when, or even if we could, ever have contact with family, they did seem confident that this third move would be the last before relocating us to Mom's choice, the Sunshine State.

This new destination would turn out to be a community called South Village—the largest mobile home park in Topeka and considered one of the nicest in all the Midwest—equipped with a large community pool, tennis courts, basketball courts, and a big, beautiful clubhouse. And, most importantly, it offered us our first feeling of a home since this whole mysterious relocation began. It would give us the feeling of community, good neighbors, and a good school district for my brother and me to attend. The only thing it couldn't give us, sadly, was a timeline. How long would we have to spend in a city with a name no one could spell? How long would it be before Mom's dream of living on the beach surrounded by ocean, sand, and never-ending sunshine finally come true?

7

SMILE, IT'S GOOD FOR YOUR TEETH

I have never shied away from any conversation that had to do with music—especially when the topic is on great songs of the seventies. Music has forever held a place in my heart and has played an instrumental role throughout my life (no pun intended). I have always felt so blessed that I had the opportunity to grow up in such an iconic decade with some of the best music ever recorded.

The seventies brought roller skating on Friday nights and Saturday afternoons to songs like Elton John's *Crocodile Rock* and Captain & Tennille's *Love Will Keep Us Together*. It was Saturday nights watching Don Kirshner's Rock Concert as the likes of Kiss and KC, and the Sunshine Band made their debuts, and Sundays meant hanging out at the White Lakes Mall with that $5 Mom would leave on the counter for us to spend on whatever we wanted. The movie *The Exorcist* scared my mom so much she had to sleep out in the living room with all the lights on, and the release of *Jaws* had me running out of the theater over the scene when the decapitated head fell out from the bottom of the boat. Though these events, and many more like them, would help mold my childhood during this great decade, there would also be some that would scar us deeply.

It was the summer of 1975, and Al had decided that owning a gas station was not enough. Going into the nightclub business was the thing to do. They were known as discotheques back then, and what a great time it was to have one. It was called Sunny Sam's, and they used the famous logo of Uncle Sam pointing his finger but scratched the original motto, "We want you for the US Army," with one of Mom's many coined phrases, "Whatever Rolls your Stone." Located on prime Topeka Boulevard real estate, it was destined for success. And, sure enough, it would become "T-Town's" hot spot. Standing room only almost every night with lines out the door waiting to get in was the norm.

The weekends were the craziest, and it was not long before this new business of ours would start taking a real toll on our home life.

The late nights with Al coming home half-drunk, complaining about how many fights he had to break up, had Mom missing a lot of sleep. And because he was known as the "tough guy nobody should mess with," he was involved in all of them. Coming home with busted-up knuckles and bloody shirts was a common occurrence, and it was almost never his blood. This was at a time when fights were handled the old-fashioned way: you took it outside. The busier a club got and the drunker the clientele became, the more fights were bound to break out. And Al just happened to be a guy who loved to fight.

One typical Friday evening, while my mom, my brother, and I were comfortably in for the night watching one of our favorite TV shows, *Quincy, ME,* we would receive an unexpected appearance through our front door. Without warning, Al came barging in unannounced and about scared us half to death.

"Surprise!" he yelled as he came into the living room. "Viv, I need to get another shirt on," he said as he removed his leather jacket, revealing a huge bloodstain covering the entire front of the brand-new shirt Mom had just bought him that afternoon. "I've got to get back to the club."

"Oh, my Goodness Al, what happened to you; are you hurt?" she asked as she popped up from the couch in an instant. "Whose blood is this?"

"Not mine," he confidently answered with a slight smirk on his face. "I had to bust a guy's nose for taking a piss on the side of our building tonight, and I hit him so hard his nose just exploded."

His face quickly turned to anger as he continued, "We threw this moron out earlier in the night, and he decides he's gonna pay me back by disrespecting my club! The prick's lucky I didn't kill him."

Mom, clearly shaken up, quickly asked Al to come to the bedroom so she could get him out of that blood-stained shirt and into another. I could hear in Mom's voice that she was just trying to get him and that shirt out of our sight, as my brother and I looked at each other in shock.

Fortunately for me, even though there were far more horrific experiences than good ones that came with owning Sunny Sam's, there was a small victory by way of something they called "Kids Night." This was one night a week that kids, ten years old and up, were allowed in with their parents to experience just what it was like to party in a real-live discotheque. And this would become one night a week for me that would leave an everlasting, life-changing impression.

The first Sunday night I spent at the hottest club in Topeka was indeed one for the record books. Despite only being nine (the ten-and-up rule was waved by default, considering I was the owner's son), you would have thought I had been hanging out in the spotlight for years. It seemed to all happen in an instant the moment Mom and I walked in the door. Denny, one of the bartenders, spotted us right away and waved us over, offering us a soda of our choice.

"What will it be, Viv? And, Bradley, how about you? We have Dr. Wells now, everybody's favorite?"

"Sure," I said, standing next to Mom, mesmerized by the atmosphere. Above the bar was the biggest painting I had ever seen, consuming the entire wall with that famous image of Uncle Sam pointing his finger and that line Mom came up with across the top and bottom, "What Ever Rolls Your Stone." As my eyes followed the art, it led me to the other side of the club, and there is where my baby blues froze. It was my first look at a real-live DJ booth. It was raised off the dance floor, with chaser lights surrounding the top and bottom, moving in rhythm to the beat of every song. If I looked hard enough to the very top of the booth, I could just barely see the head of a man with a thick mustache and tinted glasses wearing a set of huge black headphones. This was obviously the one responsible for playing all this incredible music. This man had complete control over all the energy in this room.

Mom and I sat at a table close to the action as I

absorbed into this newfound amazement. Song after song pumped through those towering PA speakers as the crowd grew bigger and bigger on that multicolor-lit dance floor. As the DJ transitioned from Head East's *Never Been Any Reason* to Elton John's *Saturday Night's Alright for Fighting*, the crowd really kicked it into high gear. You could tell they had been waiting for this moment as they cheered to the rocking sounds and packed that floor even more. This overwhelming energy I was experiencing reminded me of that same feeling I had as a young boy peeking through my bedroom door for a glimpse of all those house parties Mom would have, only times ten. Because now I was finally part of it.

"Bradley," Mom said as she tapped my arm to get my attention. "I have somebody I want you to meet."

Just as she spoke, a young lady sat down at our table next to me and said, "This must be your son Bradley that I've heard so much about." She reached for my hand. "Hi, Bradley, my name is Emily, and it's so nice to finally meet you!"

The music was so loud, I was afraid to speak, fearing she might not be able to hear me, so I just smiled and shook her hand. Mom explained that Emily was Denny's girlfriend and also one of the waitresses for the club.

"Bradley," Emily said. "If you are anything like your mom, then I know you can't wait to get out on that dance floor, so, when you're ready, I would love to be your dance partner."

Mom laughed with excitement and quickly said, "Yes, Bradley; you should get out there with Emily and shake your butt! Come on, you can do it; show us what you got!"

Just as she gave me a big smile of encouragement, KC and the Sunshine Band's *Boogie Shoes* came blasting from the speakers, and, with Emily grabbing my arm to get out there, I just couldn't bring myself to disappoint them; so, off we went!

Mom watched on as her nine-year-old son shook his booty on that dance floor like a true veteran. Moving to the beat like a youngster with some real rhythm, I began catching the attention of those dancing near me, and before I knew it, the crowd had formed a circle around us, clapping their hands and cheering us on. I was getting confident now, and, with Emily's help, we began what was known as The Bump. The crowd couldn't believe it, applauding us as we went from bumping hips to bumping knees with the help of her instruction. I could see Mom out of the corner of my eye, standing on a chair to catch the best view of this incredible moment.

After two full songs, the DJ shifted to a slow set, and we made it back to the table, met with joy and hugs from Mom and a fresh Dr. Wells for me. Emily expressed how great she thought I had done out there and then enthusiastically said, "So now that we know you can dance, Bradley, I want you to be my partner in the Bump Contest the club's having tonight!"

"What?" I replied. "Bump Contest? What's that?"

"Just do exactly what we just did out there, and you'll be fine. Dance like that, and we are sure to win!"

And sure enough, we did. And, besides the bragging rights that something like that gives a nine-year-old, I also won the Ohio Players' latest album, *Honey*, which included one of my favorite songs, Love Rollercoaster. These Sunday Kids Nights continued, and I made sure to never miss a week. Requesting songs became my favorite part besides showing off my moves on the dance floor as Emily continued to be one of my favorite partners, holding a close second to Mom, of course. My two favorite go-to requests were always Maxine Nightingale's

Right Back Where We Started From and Penny McLean's *Lady Bump*. Those were two of the many that were guaranteed to pack the dance floor.

Eventually, even on Kids Night, the fights and constant trouble would persist and, sadly, would leave the club no choice but to put an end to those Sundays for good. The troubles of this business were becoming even worse behind the scenes as the staff began to realize how self-destructive Al was becoming. Between all the drinking, bar fighting, and bad karma that this club was attracting, it was just a matter of time before it would all come crashing down.

It was late on a Saturday night, and my brother and I headed to bed after watching another great episode of Don Kirshner's Rock Concert. We had the house to ourselves as Mom had decided to go to the club to keep a closer eye on Al in hopes that she might help keep him under control. She had started doing this as much as she could while still trying to balance ten-hour shifts at the salon. Most nights, it was a success, but it was all dependent on how much he would decide to drink. And on this night, it was an epic failure.

It was well after 3 a.m. when we were suddenly awakened by loud screaming and the sound of things being broken. I heard Mom's voice in a panic, pleading, "Please, Al, stop this craziness; please, the kids are sleeping!"

"I don't give a fuck," Al screamed. "Let them wake up! Hell, go get them up, let them hear this!"

My brother and I were both up and sitting on the edge of our beds, frozen in fear. Our bedroom door was slightly cracked open, giving just enough light to barely see our silhouettes.

"Oh my God, Al, no. Please don't let them see you this way. Please, Al, will you just settle down!"

To hear Mom's voice in such panic was overwhelming to us. Finally, my brother stood up as if to head toward the door. "No," I insisted. "Don't go out there. No way! Stay in here with me, please."

Just as he backed away from the door and sat back down with me, it all stopped. Just like that. No more noise and no more screaming. We both looked at that crack of light in the door, wondering the same thing. Was he gone? Was Mom still out there? My brother shot up first and opened the door a little wider, giving himself a chance to look down the hall.

"Mom," he said, with hesitation in his voice. "Mom, are you there? Are you OK?"

Our hearts raced as we waited for a response, but something else caught our attention. A clear sound of deep sobbing was coming from the living room, and I instantly knew it was coming from Mom. I pulled the door the rest of the way open, and down the hall we went, to find Mom broken down in tears on the couch. I rushed to her side as she looked up at us, eyes swollen and pouring tears.

"Boys, I'm fine. I'm just upset right now, but I promise everything will be OK."

She began to catch her breath as she wiped the tears away from her eyes.

"But Al is very upset, and he's had way too much to drink tonight, so I need you two to get back in bed before he comes home again."

She explained that there had been several fights inside and outside the club and that Al had been a part of breaking up all of them.

"He has been out of control all night, and I don't want you boys near him when he is like this."

Just as she said that, the phone rang. Mom immediately headed to answer it.

"Hello? Al, is that you?"

The look on her face as she paused said it all. It was him, and he was clearly still a mess.

"Please, Al, don't. No, you won't. Please tell me you won't."

She paused, quickly took the phone from her ear, and hung up.

"Boys, we have to hurry. We have to find Al's guns, and we have to find them fast."

"Guns?" I yelled. "We have to find his guns?"

Following her back to their bedroom, we kept asking what was going on, but all she would say was, "We don't have time to discuss it right now; just help me find these guns."

Al had quite a collection of rifles and shotguns, as he was big into hunting but didn't own a gun cabinet; instead, he just lined them upright beside and behind his dresser. I was deathly afraid of guns and never liked looking at them, let alone having to touch them in order to get them out of the room. Mom had me grab only the ones in cases while my brother grabbed the loose rifles. She gathered the ammo, and we headed to the living room.

"Where should we put them?" I asked as we started laying them on the floor.

"Here, let's hide them behind the couch," Mom said as she started moving one side away from the wall. We ran to the other side, grabbed hold of that gold velvet classic, and joined her in getting it far enough out to fit all the rifles and shotguns neatly behind without a trace. We pushed it back against the wall and, in that moment of pause, I could feel a slight sense of relief as we all sat down on the couch together.

"OK, now," Mom sighed, "about these guns. Al is so out of control that he is threatening to come get these guns and go back out on top of the Topeka State Capitol building and start shooting people."

She grabbed our hands and pleaded again, "I know how crazy this sounds, boys, and believe me, it is, but I need you two to get back in your room and shut the door in case he really comes back to do this."

The fear in me went up tenfold as we both wasted no time getting back behind our bedroom door. As we lay in silence, my heart kept pounding as I wondered when, or even if, I would hear this maniac come through the front door. Silence would soon turn to voices, and the distinct sound of his voice became clear. Though it started off low, it wasn't long before the volume of voices exploded again, mostly led by Al's.

"Where the fuck are they?" he screamed. "You better show me where they are before I start tearing this goddamn house apart!"

Mom pleaded with him to stop the nonsense, but he was determined to find those guns and wasn't giving up until he did. Eventually, he would prevail, grabbing two of his thirty-aught-sixes with long-range telescopes and storming back out the door.

Needless to say, it was one of the scariest events of my life to date and was certainly a defining moment in how we saw this man named Al from that day forward. He went from being a man to a monster before our eyes, and that had profound implications on the relationship. Never again would I see this man in a normal light. I feared him immensely and never knew from one day to the next if, or when, he would explode again.

Fortunately, he would not carry through with his plan to turn town sniper and get his revenge on the city. His return home and a day to sober up, along with lots of apologies to Mom, would bring some temporary calm to the household. But the days of owning that nightclub with the cool name would soon end. And, in the process, he would also give up his share in the gas station to his business partner.

There were two more businesses up and running at that time, as well, so all was not lost. It seems Al had invested in a couple of Dairy Queen restaurants as the demise of the nightclub was coming near and had already begun transitioning the staff over to run them. At least these investments had some perks: free ice cream.

Sadly, neither of those endeavors would see any success, either, and would be sold off not long after their launch. Al would join up with a man he had met during the nightclub days and try his luck as a painter. At this point, the only true success had been Mom's career. She was now working for her second boss at one of the most popular salons in town. She had an enormous clientele at this point, and her boss just loved her. It was becoming evident that if Al were to continue looking for a business investment that would succeed, it only made sense to invest in Mom. She was, without a doubt, one of the best in town, and, with the size of her appointment book, she was forced to turn down more business than most stylists even had. Besides that, it was something she had always dreamed of doing and was certainly deserving of the opportunity.

So, it was done. By 1979, The Split End was born. Mom came up with the name, and I am proud to say that I designed the logo that would end up on the sign that hung above the shop. The grand opening was one of the happiest days of Mom's life and everybody, including my brother and me, was so happy for her. I was never prouder to be her son and never more excited for what we all knew would be a success.

Business would build up as word-of-mouth quickly spread through town. By this time, everybody adored this warm soul they called Viv and were more than happy to help make The Split End a smash hit. She also had been given the nickname Red by close friends, as she was known for her beautiful, bright-red hair. Though she was not a natural redhead, you would have never known it, simply because she wore that color so well. And that was certainly one of the three skills she was best known for. She was an incredible hair-color artist, one of the best at cutting a head of hair, and third—the best one of all—she had an amazing personality.

As much as her clientele counted on her to make them beautiful, they mostly just wanted to be around her, to make them laugh, and to better their day. Her smile drew you in, and nobody had one brighter. And that is how yet another phrase of hers was coined, as she so often would say, "Smile, it's good for your teeth!"

8

ONLY FIVE YEARS

Just another day at The Split End, with Mom giving
haircuts to the neighborhood kids.

I t was the start of 1980, and Mom's salon was up and
running as Al was now officially a full-time painter.
The previous summer, I had landed my first real job
washing dishes at the Village Inn Pancake House, sharing
in the strong work ethic of our household. It was an
example that was set for us at an early age. If you wanted

extra spending money, then you had to go out and earn it. And that is just what I did. It was a weekend job that paid a whopping $3.35 an hour. Back then, that was the definition of "making it" for a fourteen-year-old. It would afford me a whole lot more at the mall than the generous $5 Mom used to leave us on the kitchen counter.

I proved to be a hard worker and, after a year of busting suds, they promoted me to busboy. For thirty cents more an hour, I got to wear a bowtie, stay clean, and enjoy a lot less stress. Things couldn't be better.

And then, one Saturday afternoon, the opportunity I never even knew I was waiting on came walking through the restaurant's front door.

A friend had shown up unannounced just after the rush had died down to give me some exciting news.

"Dude, you are not going to believe where I'm working at now," he boasted as he approached the table I was wiping off.

"What, you got a new job?" I asked. "What happened to the job at Burger King?"

He laughed. "Oh man, I quit that as soon as I found out I had this job. I'm now working at the hottest nightclub in town and making $5 an hour!"

"Five dollars an hour, really?" I asked in amazement. "What nightclub are you talking about?"

"It's called Picasso and, dude, this place is unbelievable!" He went on about how there were beautiful waitresses everywhere, and they blasted great music all day and all night.

"And I can get you a job there, too, man," he bragged. "My boss is looking for one more dishwasher to fill the shifts, and I told him I knew the perfect guy for the job."

I had now stopped wiping the table as this began to sound very interesting.

"Dude, you have to take this job," my buddy said. "It's got a nightclub on one side and a restaurant on the other." He described the layout, complete with a towering DJ booth, full light shows, and a rocking sound system. My mind immediately flashed back to "Kids Night" at Sunny Sam's and how impactful that experience was for me. On weekends, after the kitchen closed, the bartenders often needed help washing glasses and asked the kitchen crew to come out front and give them a hand. And that, of course, meant we could be right out in the middle of the action.

At that point, I was sold and, without hesitation, told my friend to tell his boss that I was in. I put in my two weeks' notice at the Village Inn and was about to begin what would turn out to be a whole lot more than just a part-time dishwashing gig.

I loved this new job of mine and, from the very start, worked as hard as I possibly could to show my new boss that I was definitely an employee he could count on. It all soon paid off as he saw my potential and moved me to prep cook and then up to full line cook. This newfound love for the culinary world would really pay off at home as Mom and Al were putting in long hours and rarely home in time to cook dinner, let alone ever eat with us.

By 1982, things at home started looking quite different to me. Certainly, some of it could be attributed to adolescence and the fact that I, too, was working much of the time. I was now a sophomore in high school, and between school, work, and hanging out with friends, I was seldom home myself. When we were all home at the same time, however, there was a real sense of stress in the air. Though the relationship between my brother and Al had always been nonexistent, I had, at least in the past, tried to keep the peace between us. With scarring memories like the horrific night back in 1975, when he became a complete monster in search of his guns, or the unforgettable afternoon a short year later when he met me at the house after school holding his belt, it's safe to say our relationship was based solely on fear. The "belt event," in fact, would be the one that instilled a fear of this man so deep in me that I was never quite the same around him again.

I had done a foolish thing that day before in my fourth-grade class. I thought it would be funny to take one of the film strip containers from its boxset as we were all lined up to go home. Little did I know this was the set of film strips we were to watch the next day, so inevitably its disappearance would easily be discovered by my teacher. Even dumber was the fact that I then placed it under the school bus tire so my friends and I could watch it get crushed. After discovering what I had done, the school immediately sent a letter along, with a phone call, telling Mom and Al everything. And with that, the nightmare afternoon began.

As soon as I walked in the door and saw Al sitting on the arm of his recliner, I knew I was in trouble.

"Lock the door behind you," he barked as he stood up from the chair.

"What the hell is this letter your mom and I received this morning all about!" he yelled as he came closer to me. I stepped back. My heart raced a million miles a second.

"I don't know, Al. Why did they send a letter?" I muttered, barely able to pronounce the words.

"You know exactly why, boy! Don't you lie to me," he yelled as he started to take off his belt. "So you're a thief now? Stealing film strips from school and then destroying them?"

I stood speechless and trembling as he folded his belt in half and walked toward me.

"There will be no thieves in this house, and it's time I show you what happens when you steal." He grabbed my arm and began wailing on my backside with the heavy leather belt.

I screamed in pain with every swing. "Please, Al!" I pleaded. "Please stop. You're really hurting me; please stop!"

But he did not stop. In fact, the more I screamed, the harder he hit me. From the middle of my back down to the back of my legs and everywhere in between, he continued. Holding my arm only meant we would continue going around in circles as I tried to get away. There was a reason he had me lock the door. That became clear when my brother, returning home from school, was unable to get in. My poor brother stood helpless on the front steps, able to see everything through the sliding glass door but unable to do anything to stop it.

Though the whooping did finally end, and the welts and bruises eventually healed, the emotional scars were inflicted for life. From that day forward, I never again questioned why my brother hated this man so. The better question was simply, "Why not?"

It became clear as time went on that it just did not seem possible that this "ex-marshal" could have ever been a Lawman. We had a lot of experience around the US Marshals Service, and these officers were nothing like him. They were respectful and always concerned for our well-being. Al smoked like a chimney, drank like a fish, and cussed like a sailor. He was a walking time bomb capable of exploding at any moment. We were raised on the F-bomb by this man. The truth was that at this point, whenever my brother or I were home, we only wanted to be around Mom. And if only he was there, we made every effort to stay away. Being around Mom was the only thing that mattered to us, and that is exactly what had changed. She was not the same. We were used to always seeing Al's half-gallon bottle of rum on the kitchen counter to serve up his daily cocktails and Mom with her occasional glass of wine. But now Mom had her own half-gallon of scotch right alongside his. And though I had noticed an increase in the times I would see her holding a glass of wine, I had no idea she even drank scotch. There was a real sense of unhappiness in her, and I often thought how hard it must have been for her to live with this man, knowing how much her sons hated him and knowing down deep that they had every reason to.

It turned out that my sense of Mom's sadness was real, and it would be more than just the stress of Al's anger management issues bringing her down. She was putting in twelve-to-fourteen-hour days at the salon, as she was the primary breadwinner, and because she was so loyal to her clientele. She just refused to let up. My brother was less than a year away from high school graduation, and her precious boys were growing up faster than she was ready for. Besides all of that weighing on her heart and draining her physically, there would be something else, something that we could not have guessed in a million years and something that would have an impact certain to change our lives forever.

It was just a normal afternoon returning home from school for me. I was off work and excited to be able to throw the school books on the table, grab a bite to eat, and head on over to my buddy's house. But as I approached the door, I noticed Mom's beautiful red Corvette Roadster out front. This was a real surprise, considering she was usually never home from work before dinnertime, if not even later. I rushed in, excited to see her, and quickly noticed she wasn't out front anywhere. I looked in the kitchen and back into the living room, but no sign of her smile.

"Mom," I shouted as I looked down the hallway to her bedroom, "Mom, are you home?"

"Bradley is that you?" she replied in a somewhat somber voice coming from her room. "Yes, I'm here. Come on back and so I can see you."

Excited, I headed back to see what had brought her home from work so early. As I turned through the doorway, there she was, lying in bed under the covers in her pajamas with a look in her eyes as if she had just woken up.

Her smile lit up at the sight of me as she quickly asked, "So how's my Bradley Mark, and how was school today?"

"Fine," I answered. "And how about you, Mom? Why are you home so early today? Are you sick?"

"No, Bradley, I'm just fine," she replied as her smile faded a bit. "I'm just a little pooped out today and really just needed to get some rest."

As much as I loved having her home for the day, I couldn't help but think there was more to this than Mom just being a little "pooped out." It seemed that for her to reschedule an entire day of clients, she must have been more than just a little tired, but I was sure if that were the case, she would have certainly told me.

As we talked a little more, her eyes began to get heavy. "Mom," I said as I chuckled a bit. "You are falling asleep on me now, so I'm going to leave you to get some rest."

"OK," she said as she closed her eyes, "I love you, Bradley."

"I love you too," I replied as I stepped away and slowly closed her door.

It wouldn't be long before my brother got home, and soon after, Al would arrive. It seemed early for him to be home from work as well, but occasionally, when he did not have any side painting jobs following his shift at Brewster Place retirement home, we would, unfortunately, have to deal with these early returns. He headed straight to the kitchen to make his usual rum and Coke and then to his favorite recliner, where he assumed his normal position: footrest pulled up halfway, an immediate tilt to his seating position, and then the always predictable light-up of a cigarette.

"You boys have any plans this evening?" he asked as the smoke from his first drag came puffing out of his nostrils with each word.

I stopped in my tracks and immediately looked at my brother, who was already headed down the hallway to his bedroom, "No," I said. "I don't."

"What about your brother? Do you know if he does?" Al asked.

"No," my brother responded as he walked back into the living room. "I actually don't either, Al. Why? What's going on?"

He took another drink from his cocktail and replied, "Good because I need to take you both to the salon tonight after they close so the three of us can have a little talk."

Puzzled, we looked at each other and then back at him.

"Umm, OK. I guess we can," my brother reluctantly said. "But why do we need to go to the salon? Can't we just talk here?"

He took another big drag from his cigarette, polished off the rest of his drink, and answered, "No, this is something that only the three of us should discuss. I don't want your mother to be a part of what I need to talk to you two about."

My brother and I stood, confused. We could not think of any reason why he would need to talk to us, and certainly not without Mom being a part of it.

Finally, just as it began to get dark, Al received the call from the salon that he was waiting for, letting him know that they were closing. As soon as we stepped foot in the now dark and empty salon, I could just feel something was wrong. As Al switched on the lights and this beautifully decorated salon came into full view, I immediately thought about Mom. Everything about it captured her personality—the bright green stylist chairs (green was her favorite color) and the metallic gold and yellow wallpaper design throughout. My eyes went directly to her station and her chair, but before I could make a move, my brother quickly took it to sit down. I grabbed a chair in the station nearest hers and took a deep breath as I watched Al put down his keys.

He stood against a booth across from us and, with a look on his face that I had never seen before, asked, "So how long do you two think I'm going to live?"

Instantly, I thought he must be getting ready to tell us that he was going to die soon. It made perfect sense now why he would not want Mom to be a part of this discussion. We both went silent and just looked at each other.

He asked again, but a little differently this time. "Considering I smoke and drink and I'm out of shape and overweight, how long would you say I have left to live?"

I thought about it for a moment and replied, "I don't know, maybe 60?"

He was taken back by that and said with a chuckle, "Well, I hope I live that long."

My brother responded with a laugh of his own, and it seemed, at least for the moment, to lighten the mood.

"So, who do you think will live longer? Your mom or me?" Al asked.

Well, that might have been the easiest question we had gotten all night. I looked over at my brother, and we both almost simultaneously answered, "Well, Mom will, for sure."

"Well, of course," he agreed. "It would only make sense that she would outlive me. She's younger, has more energy, and is in much better shape."

My brother then asked the most obvious question. "So, why are you asking us this, Al? Is there something wrong with you? Are you OK?"

His face went blank, and his eyes began to squint. He paused for what seemed like an eternity before the words finally came out. "Well, there is something wrong," he trembled. "But it's not with me; it's with your mother."

My eyes froze on his face. My heart seemed to stop. I felt like I was in the Twilight Zone as I thought, *How could this be? Something is wrong with Mom? Something so wrong that Al had to bring us here to discuss it? But she was only thirty-six years old. What could possibly be so wrong?*

"You see, your mother is really sick right now, and the doctors just don't know if there is anything that they can do for her."

My brother jumped in. "What do you mean, they don't think there's anything they can do? What is wrong with her?"

"Guys, the truth is, your mother is suffering from what the doctors call cirrhosis of the liver," he continued. "What this means is that her liver has severely deteriorated over time and, according to the doctor we visited with this morning, it all started way back in

Chicago when you three got in that accident with the school bus."

"What?" I asked in complete disbelief, "You mean that accident injured her liver too?"

My mind raced back to that crash and Mom holding her blood-covered nose. I tried desperately to remember if she seemed to be hurt anywhere else, but I was blank.

"No," Al explained. "But it did result in complications with her liver. Unfortunately, during her nose operation, she contracted hepatitis C, which almost immediately began the deterioration process."

I sat, stunned at this news, and to look over at my brother and see the pain on his face was unbearable. I saw his tears roll and instantaneously began to weep. Al looked back at us, and he, too, was clearly emotional. I looked away from everything in front of me and began a deep stare into space with tears pouring down. And then it came. The news no one was ready for. Just when I thought it couldn't possibly get worse than this very moment, it did.

Al slowly sat down in front of us, appearing to be shaken by what he was about to say. "Your mom's doctor told us that because her condition had gone untreated for so long and the cirrhosis was now so severe," he paused in an attempt to pull it together, "that if she's lucky, she might live another five years."

At this point, I went numb. My heart seemed to stop beating as I slumped down in the chair. My face fell in my hands, and I began to bawl uncontrollably. I could hear my brother just a few feet away, crying out, "No way, there's just no way this can be happening!"

My brother continued to insist that there had to be something they could do for her, and there was no way she could ever leave us that soon. I just sat in a state of confusion with the words "might live another five years" echoing over and over in my head. Al tried his best to soften the blow by telling us that while she remained under the doctors' care and followed closely to the things he insisted she do, there was a chance of slowing down the deterioration process. This meant cutting back on her workload at the salon, doing all she could to ease the stress at home and, most importantly, she had to stop drinking. That certainly made me see things a bit clearer. If Mom could just listen to the doctor and do what he tells her to do, then maybe, just maybe, it could mean many, many more years with us.

As soon as we got home that night, I headed straight to my room and shut the door. As I sat on the bed, all I could think about was what to say to her. How do I approach this, and what if she doesn't even know that I know? Do I tell her I know and, if I do, am I really ready to hear how she feels about it all? As I quietly opened my door to see who was still up, I heard her voice, that soft tone coming from her bedroom. "Bradley, is that you?" she asked.

"Yes. Mom. It's me," I answered. "We're home now."

"Come back here and see me," she replied. "Come say goodnight."

As I entered the room, there she was, sitting up in bed looking wide awake with that contagiously beautiful smile. She immediately asked me to come over to her side of the bed and sit with her.

"Did you two have a talk with Al tonight?" she asked as she took both my hands in hers.

I paused for a moment and then slowly said, "Yes, we did."

Without hesitation, she quickly responded, "Now, Bradley, I want you to know that I'm not going anywhere." She looked directly into my eyes. "Now, I don't know exactly what Al told you two, but I am just fine, and this liver of mine is going to be just fine. So, I need you to promise me you are not going to worry because everything is going to be OK."

I felt my entire body exhale as I heard those comforting words.

"I have a great doctor, and he is going to take very good care of me," she continued as she held my hands tighter. She was looking at me with such sincerity that all I could think about was how much I just needed to believe her and how badly I needed all of this to go away. I felt my tears returning as she reached out her arms to pull me in for a big hug. I held her so tight as I cried like a baby in her arms while all she kept saying in my ear was, "Oh Bradley, it's OK, it's all going to be OK. I'm not going anywhere. I promise I'm not going anywhere."

We cried together that night until our noses got so snotty we finally had to take a Kleenex break. We laughed as we handed each other tissues, and it was at that moment that I decided to lose this incredible woman was just not an option. She was going to get through this, and that was all there was to it.

9

LACY JAYE

The next three years proved to be a turning point in all our lives. There comes a time in our life's journey when we need comfort—comfort from whatever is hurting us, when we need to feel better about our circumstances no matter what we must do to achieve it. This desire resonated in all four of us during this time, and we each sought it in our own way.

Al continued picking up side jobs and was rarely home before the rest of us had already gone to bed. His drinking increased, and our relationship would continue to be nonexistent. By 1982, my brother had graduated from high school and entered college. This direction helped him to stay focused on anything but Mom's health and away from all the drama that came from living with Al.

I was working thirty hours a week at the club and trying my best to manage school. However, the shifts lasted later and later, and it became harder for me to get up in the morning. I almost never made first hour, and my grades began to take a hit. The truth was, I was gradually adopting a whole new set of friends and influences. I was no longer interested in high school activities like sports or going to prom. I was much more into hanging out front in the club with the adults once my shift in the kitchen was over. This was clearly where all the excitement took place, and I always had a strong genetic connection to it all.

Yet, with a new set of friends came the inability to say no. The nightclub scene in the '80s had a unique culture, and I was quickly swept up in all that it had to offer. It was normal to witness cocaine use, whether in the public restroom or back in the storeroom by the employees. Though I was only beginning my recreational use of marijuana at that time, the nightclub culture continued to influence my decisions and slowly took priority over my responsibilities, including education.

Mom started cutting back on her work schedule, as the doctor had insisted, and even picked up an exercise class twice a week. The lightened workload gave her more free time, and that meant more sunbathing in the summer. It was my mom who taught me everything there is to know about how to get the perfect tan. It was one of her absolute favorite things to do, spending up to eight hours a day bronzing up like a coconut, no matter how hot it was. Mom's love for the sun made it easy to understand why, during our relocation process, she never gave up trying to get us to Florida. I have often thought that, down deep, she knew she might not make it there and was determined to get in as much sun time as long as she possibly could.

With my brother moved out and the reality that I wasn't far behind, Mom comforted herself with a decision that, in the end, would benefit all of us. She reached out to some friends who were avid hunters and raised Brittany spaniels. Their female had just had a litter of beautiful pups, and their owners had told Mom she was more than welcome to take a look. It evidently didn't take much convincing as she arrived home one afternoon with the most adorable Brittany pup you have ever seen. This beautiful baby girl was given the name Lacy Jaye, and though she stole the hearts of all of us, there was only one heart that Lacy would attach herself to for life. Mom and Lacy Jaye would become inseparable. She would often say they were just like "two peas in a pod."

Lacy became more than just a companion; she was like the daughter Mom never had, like soulmates destined for each other. Though it seemed crazy, it was a beautiful thing to watch. This Brittany spaniel was raised like a little human. They slept together, ate break-fast together, and even drove around in Mom's gorgeous red '75 Corvette roadster together. Lacy sat up in the passenger seat with her seat belt on, and down the road they went, top

Relaxing in her favorite chair, Mom's closest confidant and the real head of the household, Lacy Jaye.

down, music blasting, and Mom's coined phrase "Doo Dah" spelled across her personalized license plate. People looked over when they were at a stoplight and just cracked up. When they ate breakfast together, Lacy sat at the kitchen table just like Mom did, politely sitting up with all four legs on the chair and waiting patiently to be served. When Mom placed her eggs in front of her, she always waited until Mom sat down first and would not start eating until Mom did. And even though she finished way ahead of Mom, Lacy would not leave the table until she had finished as well and was ready to get up.

This amazing companion was bathed almost every day with nothing but the best in salon-grade hair care and had a coat of fur on her as beautiful as one could imagine. Nothing but the best for Mom's partner, and there was no doubt that the day Lacy Jaye was brought home was the day Mom's heart began to heal.

It was now 1984, the year I proudly graduated from high school and also the year of Van Halen's biggest selling album to date, *1984*. That summer, following graduation, I turned eighteen and had decided college was something I was just not interested in pursuing. I poured all my time into working at the club and all my free time doing just that: being free and enjoying all the perks of being a young adult and the freedom of coming and going as I pleased. Mom and Al were OK with me living at home so long as I kept them informed of my whereabouts. Early on, things were good. Mom continued to keep her workload down at the salon, and Lacy was certainly the leading lady of the household.

But when it came to the other two important orders the doctor had for Mom, she was not abiding so well. She was growing increasingly more unhappy with Al every day, and there were obvious reasons for this. Mom's shortened workload was clearly putting pressure on Al to bring in more income. Thus, the addition of more side painting jobs was a must. This kept him working long hours and away from the house on a regular basis and, in turn, kept them from spending any real time together. She carried a lot of guilt for not being able to contribute as she had been. With no one around to share her feelings with, she found more comfort in her occasional glass. Just as Lacy had helped fill the void of losing her sons to adulthood, alcohol filled the void of her broken marriage. As much as I worried about what this could mean for her health, I found it hard to say anything. And, besides that, I was just so confident that she would get through this liver crisis and never let it take her down that I refused to think about it.

By 1985, I was creating more stress around the house than Mom ever deserved. I was fully engaged in the night-club lifestyle and was not holding up my end of the bargain when it came to keeping Mom in the know of my whereabouts at all. I was often gone all night after my shifts and did not return home until late the following day. This coming and going as I pleased, using their home only as a place to sleep, was not only aggravating to them but also created suspicion as to what I was really up to. Why was I spending so much time away, and with whom? And why did I look so sleep-deprived when I finally did arrive? These questions, and many more, were about to be answered, whether I was ready for them to or not.

It was a Friday night just before 11 p.m. when I returned home from work directly after my shift. This was a first for me in a very long time, and I hoped that Mom might be pleasantly surprised. As I opened the door, she was the first one I saw, but that usual look of happiness to see me was not at all what I got. She slowly turned her head to make eye contact with me, and instantly I knew there was something very wrong.

"Hello, Bradley," she said softly as she turned her head back down toward the floor. I stopped in my tracks at the sight of her sadness and immediately wondered if Al was in the room with her.

"Bradley, get in here," Al barked as I remained frozen in the entryway and out of his line of sight.

Mom looked back up at me and, with the saddest eyes, said, "Bradley, come on in here. We both need to have a talk with you."

My mind was racing as I slowly stepped into the living room just far enough to see Al sitting in his chair. All I kept thinking was, what on earth could this possibly be about?

"I said get in here!" he yelled, "All the way in here so I can see you!"

I stepped into the room a little further and nervously asked, "What's wrong, Mom? What is going on?"

"Don't look at her," he demanded. "Look at me!"

My heart did a triple beat as I quickly looked back at him.

"What in the hell is this little piece of paper, full of white powder, you have folded up in your shirt pocket hidden inside your bedroom closet?" he asked.

I stood motionless as the question sent me into panic mode. I knew exactly what he was talking about and now understood clearly what was happening.

"Is it cocaine?" he asked.

I stood trembling in silence.

"I said, is it cocaine!" he yelled.

I looked back at Mom only to see the most disappointed look on her face that I had ever seen.

"Yes," I answered, "Yes it is."

I watched as Mom's face fell into her hands as she began to weep. I could hear her mumbling, "Oh Bradley, Oh Bradley Mark, why?" she kept saying under her breath. "How could you do this?"

That question from her, I just could not answer. How could I have done this? I was just eighteen, caught up in the nightclub life, and was doing the same as everyone else around me: partying. Cocaine was very much the popular drug of choice, and it didn't take long once I began attending the employee after-hours parties to figure that out. Though it was strictly recreational to me and seemed harmless at the time, I still always knew that keeping it a secret was paramount. And as I stood there, witnessing Mom's devastation, that became all too clear.

"Your mother and I will not live with drugs under our roof," Al said. "So I think it's time you pack your shit and get out."

I looked right at Mom and saw her look of helplessness. I knew in my heart she did not want to do this, but I also knew she had no choice. The damage was done, and there was no turning back. Al had the final say, and that was it. The decision to kick me out was made, and no one was sadder about it than Mom. I had hurt her deeply, and I was not proud of it. Though it was incredibly hard for her to do, it just had to be done. I needed to take responsibility for my actions, and nothing was going to change until I did.

Within a few days, and with only a box of clothes and my skateboards, I moved in with a bartender from the club on a temporary basis. Al had refused to let me have anything else to start out my new life. Neither my bed nor my dresser were allowed to come with me. Not a spoon or a fork, not a cup or dish. According to him, those things did not belong to me and were only mine to use if I were still living at home. Though not surprising to me, considering the circumstances surrounding my departure, it still hurt Mom very much that she was not able to help me the way she really wanted to.

From there, I continued to apartment-hop a total of three more times—all in the same apartment complex, so moving was not a challenge. I eventually left Picasso's after five long years for an opportunity to become kitchen manager of a club called the Green Parrot, which at that time was the most popular nightclub in town. This transition not only represented a chance for me to keep growing in the industry, but it also marked a time in my life that would change everything I ever knew.

Mom periodically came to visit me there, and I'd love that. Everybody soon knew who she was, and they too loved to see her smile just as much as I did. Though Mom and I never spoke again about the night I was kicked out or about what they found in my room, I always sensed that she was very concerned with how I was doing and what I was up to.

"Bradley Mark," she often said. "You look tired. I can see it in your eyes. Are you getting enough sleep? Are you keeping your nose clean?"

With a laugh, I always assured her I was. But she knew better. She could always tell when something was wrong just by looking into my eyes. She always told me she knew me like a book, and she was right. I have always been proud to say that she and I were the original "two peas in a pod."

10

TRUTH BE TOLD

W hen you work in the club business long enough, you begin to meet and know a lot of people. And many of those you get to know you tend to see all the time. You might say you see them on a regular basis. Thus, they become your "regulars." And because we had so many of these regulars at the Parrot, I would often see the same customers at the bar all day, every day.

There was one customer in particular who always stood out to me. His name was Steve, and though I was never sure why, this man always caught my attention. It might have been his stature, as he was a very tall and stout man. Or maybe it was because I also seemed to catch his attention, as well. We would stare at each other at times, and it seemed a little strange. He was the definition of a "bar regular," as he was there most every day and on a first-name basis with everybody.

Steve was given the VIP treatment for his commit-ment, which meant he could run a tab for a week at a time or more, and the bar never worried about his credit. This man never missed his time to pay up and was always very generous with the tips. Whenever I would come out to the bar, we would always say our hellos and, if he had eaten, I would always make sure everything was good for him.

One afternoon following the end of my shift, as I headed out to the bar to say goodbye to the staff, I caught Steve out of the corner of my eye, looked up to say hello, and noticed him gesturing me to come sit with him. This was surprising, considering I had never actually sat down with this man for a conversation. If there was one thing about Steve, it was that he was a noticeably quiet man. He kept to himself, enjoyed his cocktails, and it seemed the more he drank, the quieter he got. As intimidated as I was, I made it over and sat on the empty barstool next to him.

He started the conversation by complimenting the great turkey and Swiss sandwich I had made for him that day. After some small talk, he turned back down to his drink and appeared to pause in thought. I started to think that he had called me over merely to compliment my food, and that just didn't make any sense.

He looked back up and with a slight smile said, "I just have to tell how much I enjoy seeing your mom when she comes in here to see you."

"Oh wow," I said. "Did you see her today, Steve? She came in earlier to see me?"

"I sure did," he answered, "That Vivien is really something special, Bradley, and I have always thought the world of her."

As soon as he referred to her as Vivien, I was taken back for a moment. Though I knew that some of those I worked with knew her name, I was a little surprised that he did. My mind immediately went to the few instances I had seen her sitting next to him at the bar and guessed that she must have introduced herself.

Steve then asked me something that completely

rocked me back in my chair. He asked if she was still married to Al. There was no reasonable way that he could have known anything about her marital status, let alone who she was married to, unless someone had told him.

"How did you know she was married to Al?" I quickly asked. "Do you know him or something?"

He gave me a chuckle and said, "Do I know Al?" He paused. "Yes, you could say that. I have actually known Tubby for many, many years now."

I heard the name Tubby, and I lost my breath. It was a nickname Al had been given a long time ago that I had only heard used by the Marshals Service officers back in the early days of our relocation. There was simply no way Steve could have referred to him as that unless he knew our story.

"How did you know his nickname was Tubby?" I asked. "Were you a marshal in Chicago too?"

He looked confused and replied, "A marshal in Chicago? What are you talking about?"

He turned his chair toward me and asked, "Did he and your mom ever tell you why you moved here from Chicago?"

"Oh, you mean about Al having to arrest one of his good friends for stealing a car?" I replied, "Yes, they told us all about how this friend Charlie began threatening his life after the arrest, and it forced the Marshals Service to transfer us here."

Steve looked at me in shock. He paused for a moment, took a drink, and replied, "So Tubby told you he was a marshal working for the feds?"

He began to chuckle for a moment, and then his face went cold. He looked at me straight in the eye and said, "Bradley, what I am about to tell you must never be repeated, and I mean never! Do you understand?"

My eyes grew as big as saucers as I instantly responded, "Yes, sir, of course."

"I mean it, son. If you repeat a word of what I am about to tell you, I will march you right back to that kitchen and stick your head inside the deep fat fryer, and I won't think twice about it!"

I held my hands up. "I promise Steve, not a word."

He began by telling me that everything my brother and I were told was simply not true. He said not only was Al not a marshal, he was actually the crook stealing the cars. The whole thing about having to arrest his friend and then his friend responding by threatening Al's life was completely backward. The truth was, Al and Charlie were stealing those cars together for a syndicate of the Chicago mafia. This is something they had been doing together for a long time. They were a team and had a lot of success working together. Al evidently would handle casing out the vehicles while Charlie would hot-wire them.

Steve said that Al had gotten careless on more than one occasion, had been pulled over driving these cars and spent a couple of nights in jail.

My mind instantly raced back to that weekend in Hazel Crest, when Mom was absent for multiple days. Could that have been what really happened? Was she actually put in jail with Al?

Steve went on to explain that it was during the following traffic stop that not only led to his final arrest but forced him into a decision that would change the rest of his life and ours.

"The day Al got pulled over by himself," Steve said, "he completely folded. The truth was, he was caught once again red-handed and just knew when the mafia bailed him out this time, it would only be to kill him. So he cracked."

Steve said Al immediately began confessing to what he was up to and spared no detail. The craziest part, according to Steve, was the officer who pulled him over was only doing so because of a bad taillight. Al was so quick to confess, however, the officer never got a chance to speak.

"So, yes," Steve confirmed. "There were marshals involved all right, but not for the reasons you two were given. They came into the picture because Al chose to testify and become the state's witness against the mafia in exchange for a new life and new identity."

According to Steve, Al not only requested full immunity and a fresh start but also asked to keep all the dirty money he had earned for his work stealing cars for the mob.

At this point, I was oblivious to what was going on around me. I was in complete shock and focused only on Steve's face and the incredible words that were coming out of his mouth. So much for wondering where all the capital came from to buy all those early businesses, I thought.

According to Steve, the feds reluctantly agreed under the condition that he set up his partner, Charlie, to steal another vehicle with him. They would choose a time and place to meet, Charlie would hot-wire the car, and once it started, Al was to handcuff him to the steering wheel and inform him that he was under arrest for grand theft.

And so, it was at that point that Charlie, Al's longtime friend, and business partner, would actually threaten him, telling him that he had just made the biggest mistake of his life and was now, most definitely, a dead man.

So much to take in, and so many questions were

finally answered. What I was hearing was beyond my comprehension. All I kept thinking was how on earth could this normally quiet man I was sitting with at the bar know all this? And how could Mom have knowingly kept this from us for all these years and not been a complete wreck inside? Steve would explain just how he knew all this, as there was evidently more to Al's job than just stealing cars and chopping them up at that so-called "body shop," where he so often took me.

"Al would often have to drive across state lines with the stolen vehicles," Steve continued. "And occasionally, he was instructed to meet up with guys like me."

"Guys like you," I repeated. "You mean you stole cars too, Steve?"

"Shh, not so loud, son," he directed. "No, I was not a sneaky little car thief like Tubby. I handled the real business of the mob."

I began to feel frightened as he spoke, not knowing what he could have possibly meant by that.

"We would meet up on many occasions," Steve continued. "We rarely spoke, and when we did, it was strictly business."

He told me that Al had a real chip on his shoulder and that none of the crew liked working with the one they called Tubby. He added that it was arrogance that probably got him caught in the first place. Steve said he would then give him one, sometimes two bags, and it was Al's job to dispose of them with no questions asked.

"Bags? Bags of what?" I asked.

"Bradley," Steve said as he chuckled. "I can tell you they weren't groceries. And I can also tell you that they weren't alive, if you know what I mean."

He leaned his eyes toward mine with an ice-cold stare, and I knew exactly what he meant. This seemingly gentle man everyone adored at the bar was once a hitman for the Chicago mafia. He, too, was doing the syndicate's bidding, but on a much larger and much more dangerous scale.

"Son, I think you should know this petty car thief's testimony cost many people involved their lives," Steve continued. "And it all happened very quickly. Within twenty-four hours of your disappearance, that chop shop exploded with everybody inside. And his buddy Charlie was shot dead on his front porch the very day the mob bonded him out of jail."

He then leaned even closer and said, "And I'm certain that Tubby's admissions had everything to do with the Feds eventually catching up with me."

Needless to say, I was speechless. I left the bar that day stunned and shaken. The drive home was a blur. It was a conversation I almost wish would have never taken place. But it did, and now the only question was what to do with it. Steve made it abundantly clear I was to never repeat what I had just heard to anybody. And that meant not even Mom—the only sole I would ever want to share this with anyway.

I went home to my apartment and spent the rest of the evening pondering it over and over in my head and heart. I knew that if I were to tell her, she would never repeat it, but I also knew that telling her could certainly hurt her very much. A secret that she had kept from me my entire life to that point was now revealed to me by a man at a bar. And any chance of her being the first to tell me of such a devastating truth on her terms was no longer possible.

11

ALL SO CLEAR NOW

I n the fall of 1985, I decided to share with Mom this new truth that I had been given. This was also the defining year of my love for the great "hair band" music of the decade. From Mötley Crüe to Whitesnake, Dokken to Quiet Riot, and Ratt to Bon Jovi, not to mention the soon to come, long-awaited introduction to "Van Hagar," I jumped full force into "Hair Nation."

And in my support of this nation, I, too, had what I like to refer to as "forty pounds of Bon Jovi curl." I have always credited my mom for allowing me to wear that rocking head of hair. She strongly supported my look all through high school, so long as I kept it healthy and clean. True words spoken from a truly great hairdresser, and it never hurts when that great stylist is your mom.

The evening began with a knock at the front door of my apartment. I rushed to open it because I couldn't wait to see her smiling face.

"Mom," I cried as my arms opened as wide as the door to welcome one of her cherished hugs.

"Oh, Bradley Mark," she sighed as she squeezed me tight. "It's so good to see you!"

I wasted no time closing the door behind us and asking her what she thought of the apartment.

"I just love it," she answered with enthusiasm. "You and your roommate keep everything so nice and clean, Bradley. I just love it."

It warmed my heart to hear her say that, and while I watched her smile get bigger as she looked around, I knew that she was more than proud of how I was living. The brief tour brought us to the kitchen, where I made us a couple of ice waters and then sat up on the counter in preparation for my unfolding of Al's real identity in this relocation program as I now understood it.

"Mom, I have something I really need to ask you about," I said as she stood next to me in the kitchen. "Something a man who said he knew you told me at the club last week."

"Oh," she replied. "Who was this man who said he knew me?"

"Steve," I answered. "Steve Winters. He said he knew both you and Al. He also told me that he knew the real reason why we were relocated from Chicago."

Mom's eyes said it all. Her expression was one of shock and then devastation.

"Is it true, Mom? Is it true that Al was a car thief for the mafia?"

Her eyes slowly blinked, and as they contacted mine again, she softly said, "Oh my gosh, Bradley, is that what he told you?"

"Yes," I answered. I could feel her heart breaking. "And he told me a whole lot more than that. Like, how Al got arrested twice while driving stolen vehicles, and that's really how this whole relocation thing ever happened in the first place."

I sat on the counter and focused on Mom's reaction, hoping she would counter with a denial. Instead, she paused, took a deep, sobering breath, and said,

"Bradley, I can't imagine how you must have felt hearing those things from Steve."

She reached her hands out to hold mine and then continued, "Yes, I do know of this man at the bar, and I never, ever would have wanted you to hear the story from anybody but me."

"So, it's true, Mom? Al was really a car thief for the mob, and all that talk about him being a federal marshal was just a lie?"

At the moment she heard the word "lie," her eyes began to tear. I felt so bad for saying it like that, but I couldn't undo it at that point.

"Please, Bradley," she pleaded as she squeezed my hands tighter, "understand that it was never my intention to lie to either one of you. Never in a million years. But only to protect you two from a very dangerous situation."

I could not imagine what keeping a secret of that magnitude must have been doing to her all these years, but I could feel that she welcomed the opportunity to take it all off her heart. She began helping me understand each part of what unfolded during those early events in Hazel Crest leading up to our departure from Chicago.

"It is true what Steve has told you, Bradley. Al was stealing cars for the mafia, and he kept that a secret from all of us."

She looked me straight in the eyes and continued, "and I promise if I had ever thought that he was involved in anything criminal, I would have never pursued a relationship with him."

"So, did you actually get arrested with him driving a stolen car?" I asked. "Steve said he thought you went to jail over that."

"Yes, I did," Mom reluctantly answered. "We were both put in jail on suspicion of driving a stolen vehicle on a Friday and released the following Monday."

She continued, "And I remember so vividly, Bradley Mark, how worried you were when we finally arrived home that morning. I do remember wanting to tell you two the truth but knew you could never be ready for such a thing."

She went on to explain that although they had been pulled over once before, it was this stop that exposed all the secrets and lies. My heart pounded as she told the story, and I could not stop thinking about how hard this must have been for her.

"I had a lot of soul searching to do, Bradley," she admitted. "And with that came the reality that we had to get away from this man. I was going to have to divorce him, and that was all there was to it."

She said she confided in her best friend, Danna, to help make this plan a reality. But before it ever had a chance to come to fruition, something even worse happened.

Just a few short weeks after Al came clean to Mom, this crook was once again pulled over by the police. This time he was all by himself and knew for certain this was it.

"Oh, man," I sighed, "Steve did tell me there was a third arrest, Mom, and that Al confessed on the spot to everything."

"Yes, he did," Mom replied, "And once he did that, the three of us were left with no choice. Al cut a deal to stay out of prison, and that meant testifying against the mob and all those criminals he worked for."

She went on to confirm everything Steve had told me at the bar. She also explained how real the threat was that Charlie made to Al. And even though the US Marshals Service had given us the option to cut ties with this crook and stay in Chicago, they strongly urged Mom to think about her safety and that of her boys.

"Bradley," she said. "The only thing that ever mattered to me was you two. Keeping you safe was all that I cared about, and if that meant leaving with him to accomplish that, then it was just something we were going to have to do."

Her lips tightened as tears began to well up in her eyes. "And I never wanted to lie to you boys or intentionally keep anything from you., Ever. But once the decision to relocate was made, the rest was all dictated by the Marshals Service and all those men who were protecting us."

I dropped from the counter and wrapped my arms around her as tight as I possibly could.

"Oh, Mom," I moaned as I began to cry with her. "I completely understand, and I love you so much!"

There was no denying that we both felt relief that the secrets she had held so long were finally out in the open. I forgave her without hesitation and, as our tears slowed, assured her that I had not and would not share what I knew with my brother.

"Oh, thank you, Bradley," she replied. "I do want to be the one who tells him. And, speaking of your brother, he has been talking a lot lately about wanting to see your father. I'm just curious whether you have had any of these same thoughts."

"You mean our real father?" I asked. "Wow." I paused,

"No, not at all. In fact, I don't even remember what he looks like."

She gave a little smile and said, "You were very young, Bradley Mark, and I know that your brother remembers a whole lot more about him than you do."

She explained that if we ever decided to see our dad, it was important that we take every precaution to keep our location in Topeka a secret.

"I want you to remember, Bradley, that your father only knows that one weekend you two were at the house in Hazel Crest, and the following weekend you weren't. He has no idea what happened to you two and is most certainly still very angry about all of this."

She then shared a story of an altercation that had taken place between Al and our father that helped put things in perspective.

"One Sunday afternoon," she said, "after your father had dropped you boys off, Al called him out of his car and into the front yard for a talk. They immediately began shouting at one another, and before I could blink, they started throwing punches."

She described a scene with Al standing over our father after beating him badly and yelling, "And, mark my words, you prick: your kids are going to be my kids someday!"

I stood, stunned. "Wow. So they have always hated each other?"

"Yes, they have," she answered, "and us having disappeared like that has only made it worse, I'm sure."

She paused for a moment, took a deep breath, and said, "Now, Bradley Mark, I want you to know something that I believe is very important for you to remember."

She took my hand and looked me straight in the eyes. "I need you to know that I left your father for a reason. He was an unfaithful man who drank too much and was very verbally abusive to me."

She explained that he was immature and just not ready to be married. She said he would often go down to the basement and take money from the cash register in her salon to go out drinking with the boys. More often than not, he would stay out all night with other women, leaving her home alone to take care of us.

"The truth is, Bradley, your father was a real asshole."

My jaw instantly dropped as I heard that word come out of her mouth. Mom rarely cursed.

"Just promise me that if you ever do decide to meet your father again that you not get your hopes up. I would never want to see you hurt or deeply disappointed if it turns out that he hasn't changed."

"I really doubt that I am ever going to have any interest in meeting him, Mom," I said, "but if that day ever comes, I will make sure that I am careful about keeping our location a secret, and I promise I won't get my hopes up."

She opened her arms to me, and we hugged each other once more. I could hear her begin to cry again as she squeezed me tighter.

My mother had become an even greater soul in my eyes now that I understood what she had gone through and how she chose to handle it, never giving up on her most important objective: keeping her boys safe. She had walked away from everything she ever knew and from everyone for whom she deeply cared, just to keep us safe. And that is the purest definition of unconditional love a son could ever ask for.

12

'PROMISE TO POLISH IT EVERY DAY'

I n March of 1986, I received a phone call that changed the direction of my life forever. My brother was on the other end with panic in his voice as he explained that Mom had been rushed to the hospital and was losing lots of blood. I felt my heart stop as I froze in silence. My brother could sense my panic and immediately told me to stay put until he could come over to pick me up.

When we arrived at the hospital, the desk staff informed us Mom had already been taken to preop. Al was standing outside that room and told us we had just missed her as he pointed to the Plexiglas window behind him. There she was, lying still in her surgery cap, surrounded by nurses getting her ready for what would turn into a long night of fear and anxiety. We stood at that window in hopes that she might see us.

Within minutes, a nurse came out to the hall. "And you must be Vivien's sons," she said as she pulled down her surgical mask. "Follow me, this way," she instructed.

We followed her in as my brother went to Mom's side first. I stood about ten feet from her and struggled to take it all in. The nurse stood by me as I remained deep in shock.

"Your mother has been asking about you two," the nurse said. "In fact, she's not stopped talking about you guys since she arrived."

"She hasn't," I replied as my mouth trembled.

"She insisted that I let you two see her before she goes in to surgery."

At that moment, it all became too much for me, and I buckled down in tears.

"Now, now," the nurse gently said as she put her arm around me, "It's OK. We are going to take good care of her. Don't you worry. Your mother is very strong, and I know she would want you to be just as strong now."

Her words were comforting, and I knew she was right. I couldn't let Mom see me like this. I had to be strong and not let her see these tears. So, I opted to stand back with the nurse until it was time for Mom to be moved into surgery.

The waiting room was eerily quiet and still. My brother and I sat together across from Al and some of Mom's close friends. Nobody really spoke as the clock slowly ticked away. I could feel the fear all around me. Back and forth the nurses went—up and down the hallway with IV poles of fresh blood in their possession. In the midst of all of this, a man walked into the waiting room. He was a tall gentleman wearing all black and sporting a clerical collar.

"Hello there," he said as he walked closer to all of us. "I'm looking for Al. Is he here with us?"

"Yes, I am," Al quickly responded as he stood to shake the pastor's hand.

"Al, I'm Pastor James, a friend of Vivien's. I came as soon as I received the call. How is she doing?"

Al offered him a seat and began explaining the severity of the situation. I looked on as their voices lowered. I had no idea what to think of this. A pastor shows up while Mom is undergoing emergency surgery, and that is somehow a good thing? I only knew it to mean that this was the end, this was the moment of truth. The priest was here to give her last rites. This just couldn't be happening. He soon walked over to us and asked if he could sit down.

"I've been looking forward to meeting these sons that Vivien keeps bragging about," he said with a smile. "She goes on and on about you two all the time during our talks."

The pastor went on to explain that they had been getting together for conversation and prayer for several months. He said that she was looking for clear guidance through a very difficult time. As he spoke, the reality hit me like a shot to the heart. Only she knew how sick she really was, and she had to find out what to do alone— what to do if she really didn't make it and how to prepare us if the end was inevitable. The pain of that thought overwhelmed me, and the tears began to fall once again.

Suddenly, a voice fell into the room.

"Excuse me for the interruption. May I please speak with Vivien's husband?"

All eyes rose to see a surgeon standing before us.

"That's me," Al spouted as he rose from his seat. "I'm Alex. How is she, doctor?"

"She is doing very well considering," he continued. "She had lost a lot of blood, and it was touch and go for a while, but Viv is a real fighter, and I am happy to say she is now stable."

A sigh of relief filled the room as everyone took a huge exhale. Against all odds, and while her pastor joined us in support, Mom had made it! And, as the doctor went on to tell us, it was like a miracle he had never witnessed before.

On my way home from the hospital that night, my brother and I shared our hearts with each other. As we reflected on what had just taken place, I felt that regardless of our victory that evening, her precious liver was clearly in bad shape. To lose that much blood in that short amount of time meant this most vital organ was simply failing her. The conversation Al had sat us down for over four years earlier was now playing out in real time. Could her doctors be right? Had she not followed their orders well enough? Was their diagnosis correct? In this moment, it seemed so.

The next morning, I awoke to a soft knocking at my bedroom door.

"Dude, wake up, your mom is on the phone," my roommate whispered.

I jumped up, startled from the knock, as I tried to replay what I thought he had just said.

"Hey, man," he repeated as he pushed open my door. "Your mom is on the phone and wants to talk to you!"

"What?" I replied in disbelief. "She's calling me?"

I couldn't believe it. Less than twenty-four hours after her operation, she was strong enough to call me herself. I quickly jumped out of bed and grabbed the phone

"Mom, is that you?" I asked, desperate to hear her voice.

"Yes, Bradley. I am just fine," she replied softly. "I am still here in the hospital but feeling much better since you saw me yesterday."

When those words hit me, my heart filled with joy.

"Bradley," she continued with a hint of sadness in her voice. "I want you to know that I saw you crying with the nurse yesterday, and it just broke my heart."

There was a long pause as those words sunk in.

"I want you to understand something, and I don't want you to ever forget this. Bradley Mark, I am not going anywhere, and I promise you that we are going to beat this liver thing. I have a great doctor now, and I told him if he has to get me a new one, then that's just what we'll have to do!"

She started to laugh a little and said, "And I told him when he does, I promise to polish it every day!"

I couldn't help but laugh as my eyes filled with tears of joy. Only Mom, with her unique sense of humor, could have come up with that line. And, as crazy as that might have sounded, I knew she meant every word. That is simply why everybody loved her so much. She had a way of taking the worst of any situation and turning it into a positive, turning times of sadness into moments of pure joy just by making you laugh. She had done it again with me and managed to heal my heart and cast out any doubt or fear that she would let this illness take her away.

YOUR HAIR LOOKS GREAT

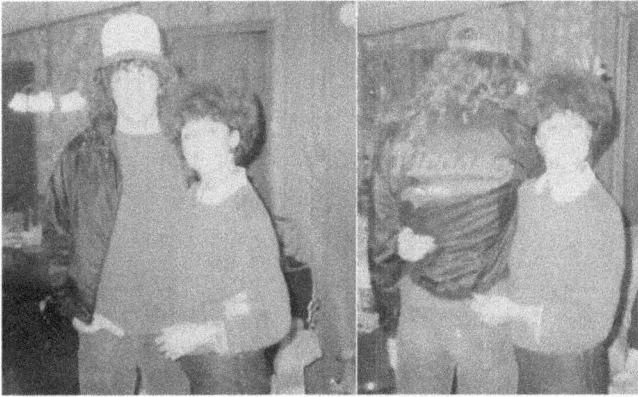

Mom always loved a good photo-op, especially when she could
show off my hair and, as she put it, "Bradley's cute little butt!"

B y the end of May 1986, it was becoming clear that
Mom's condition was not improving, and her need
for a liver transplant was vital. The problem was mom
had not yet met the criterion needed to get put on the
donor list. Because she was so young, she had not reached

the stage required for transplant eligibility known as "end-stage liver disease." Basically, it meant that unless you were on death's door and were no longer seeing results from medical treatments, you stood no chance of getting on the list. Sadly, even if she got on a list, there were no guarantees that she could survive the wait.

In the days that followed, there would be nothing more that Mom's doctor and his team could do. It seemed that all the therapies and antibiotics they had at their disposal were just not enough to keep her condition from worsening. The decision was made that in order to get her the best possible treatments and the best chance at a new liver, she would need to be airlifted to the University of Minnesota in Minneapolis. I received a call at work that morning informing me of the decision and was told if I wanted to see her off, now was the time. I was trembling as I hung up the phone and just stood in place at the end of the bar, lost in my own thoughts. I couldn't seem to come back into the here and now. I snapped back into reality when I heard a voice from the other side of the bar. It was one of my coworkers calling my name. Startled, I answered back and realized I had to go. I told the opening bartender what was going on as I rushed straight out the door and straight to St. Francis Medical.

As I entered Mom's room, I was almost afraid to look toward her bed right away. I was afraid of how she might look, and I did not want her to see me cry. A nurse by her side looked up and immediately nudged Mom.

"Viv, look who's here?" the nurse said.

Mom, lying partially on her side, looked up and that beautiful smile appeared instantly.

"Bradley Mark, get over here and let me see you."

Her voice warmed my heart as I made it over to her

side of the bed. The sun was shining through the window, and everything seemed to glow around her. She looked so much better than I had feared, and she seemed so calm. She was bragging to the nurse about how handsome I was and telling me how great my hair was looking. She asked me to come closer so she could feel it.

"So who's doing your hair now Bradley?" she asked as she held my long locks.

"June's still doing it Mom," I answered with a smile.

"Well, it looks great, and you make sure you tell June she is doing a great job."

I laughed and said I would. She let go of my curls and then she made me a promise. She promised that we were going dancing as soon as she got back. She made it clear that once she got this new liver, she would be as good as new, and I'd better be ready to cut a rug! We laughed as we held each other's hands, and I told her I was definitely holding her to it.

It would soon be time for the medical team to get Mom prepped for her journey as the thunderous sound of the helicopter landed on the hospital roof above us. I did not want to let her go and she knew it. She held my hand as long as she could, and then, with her eyes beginning to well up, said, "Bradley, it's OK. As soon as they fix me up, I'm coming right back home."

She blinked slowly and then said, "And please take care of your brother. He was here earlier, and he's not doing well with this at all. Make sure you tell him what I told you about our dancing."

I smiled and assured her I would as I left her side to make room for the nurses.

Days followed, with no word on how things were going in Minnesota. As those days quickly turned to weeks, some positive news came. Mom was doing well enough to have visitors, first from my brother and then me.

It all started very well as my brother flew up and spent a couple of quality days sitting bedside and walking the halls when doctors allowed. He returned in good spirits, and I was told to stand by for word on when I could come up. Then we received word that Mom had taken a turn for the worse as more infections were once again her enemy. She asked that I not see her that way, and it was decided that my flight be put on hold. In the meantime, we remained hopeful, knowing she was in the best of care with the best technology at her disposal.

On June 30, 1986, my brother and I celebrated his twenty-second birthday together, and what a night it turned out to be! We met up after I got off work at the club and stayed there for a couple of drinks. We then proceeded to paint the town, hitting all our favorite bars and clubs with only one intention: celebrate the moment. And celebrate we did! We ended up back where we had started, closing the Green Parrot, before my brother took me back home to the Cambridge house and dropped me off.

We never discussed Mom that night or anything that would have dampened our mood. It was all about being together and celebrating. That spirit ran into the next day, though a bit on the hungover side. I felt re-energized about everything and ready to take on whatever came my way.

I wrapped up my shift at work that evening, feeling the effects of the previous night's endeavors. I got home and fell right into my favorite chair as my roommate welcomed me home. I sensed the start of a cold coming on, and my roomie suggested a hot toddy to make me feel better. He said I would sleep like a baby, and though I had never heard of such a thing, I quickly took him up on the offer. I drank it down and, before I knew what hit me, I was out.

The next thing I remember is my roommate shaking my shoulder to wake up. I opened my eyes and realized that I was still in the same place in my chair, work clothes on, and in my shoes. It was like a dream as I heard him say, "It's for you," as he held the phone in front of me.

"She says her name is Collette, and it's important."

Startled, I looked at the clock and saw it was now 1:30 a.m. My heart raced with panic as he said the name, Collette. She was a dear friend of Mom's, and it didn't make any sense why she would be calling me—especially at this hour. I took the phone and put it to my ear. I began to hear her words, and the next five minutes on that telephone would define the rest of my life in ways that I could never imagine.

On July 1, 1986, at approximately 11:20 p.m., at the age of forty-one, Vivien Lee McDade lost her battle to liver disease. That call with Collette has remained a moment frozen in time, deep in my mind and heart. We all lost that day. The world lost a one-of-a-kind woman. It was a loss felt by everyone she ever touched and by anyone who was fortunate enough to have ever met her. I was riddled with overwhelming pain for hours as my roommate tried his best to help me through it. Eventually, my breakdown eased long enough for my swollen eyes to finally close.

My eyes would eventually open again to the bright sunshine casting through my bedroom window. I looked up with excitement, thinking it was again time to get out and work on that suntan. For a brief second, it felt just like another day until my new reality hit me and knocked me back into bed.

Please tell me I am waking up from a bad dream! No, please tell me!

But, no, I was not. These bricks on my chest taking the wind from me were real. From that moment forward, Mom was gone. The chance for me to hold her hand in Minnesota one last time was over. The phone was no longer going to ring with her on the other end, assuring me she was just fine. And there would certainly be no chance of ever getting that dance she promised. These were just some of the many painful thoughts going through my head as I laid in bed, staring out the window that sorrowful summer morning.

In the days that followed I spent much of my time in that very place—curled up, motionless, just staring out my bedroom window. The agony of losing her had completely consumed me. How could this have happened to such an amazing soul? And why? And what was I supposed to do now? Nineteen years old, an entire life-time ahead of me, and I was now expected to do it all without her. It just did not make any sense and my mind, body, and soul were devastated.

Things began to move quickly, it seemed, after the tragic news of Mom's passing. Al had remained in Minneapolis as he needed to make many decisions regarding her funeral. One of the most important deci-sions was what to do with her body. Unbeknownst to us, there had been conversations between Al and her. She wished to be cremated. It seemed in character for Mom, dreading the thought of being underground and eaten by all those bugs. More than a week went by before Al arrived back in Kansas with Mom's remains, and the funeral date was set.

Mom would be laid to rest on Saturday, July 12, at 12:30 p.m. in the service building of Mount Hope Cemetery. That morning, my brother and I met at the house to prepare for a day we would most certainly never forget. I quickly discovered that we were not the only ones experiencing tremendous grief that morning. It wasn't long after we arrived that everybody realized Lacy Jaye was nowhere to be found. We all checked room to room, with no sign of Mom's soulmate. As the time neared for us to leave and still no sign of Lacy, tension and anxiety grew. Al was adamant that we could not leave until we knew she was OK. I decided that as hard as it was for me to go in there, I would check Mom's room one more time.

I walked in, this time determined to stay as long as I needed in hopes that with more focus, I would find Lacy Jaye. I stood on the side of Mom's bed, looking down at all her favorite wigs setting neatly on wig heads across her dresser. I felt such a presence of her in that room. It almost brought me to my knees with anguish as I kneeled to make it to the edge of Mom's side of their waterbed. I laid back on the comforter, and that's when I felt it. Along with the water moving me around, there was this feeling that I was laying on something, something under the blankets that sort of felt like a pillow. Then, at that very moment, the discreet sound of a whining animal came through. It startled me, so I popped back up and felt the top of the comforter. The more I ran my hands across this lump in the bed, the warmer it felt, and the more I could hear the soft whimpering.

I quickly pulled back the covers, and my heart melted at what I saw. There was Lacy Jaye, lying on her side, pressed deep into the sheets, positioned in the very spot that Mom would sleep every night. It became perfectly clear that this little lady, who was far more human than dog, knew her best friend was never coming home. And, just like the rest of us, her little heart was broken.

That day at Mount Hope Cemetery would mark the end of one era and the start of a new one in our young adult lives. What we could not have imagined was the surprise waiting for us outside in the parking lot.

After the service, we both had decided to go for a walk to see where Mom's ashes would be kept. On our way back, we were greeted by a staff member who told us there was a gentleman at the front door asking to see us. Not thinking much of it, we both headed toward the entryway, and as we got closer, I noticed a man who looked a bit out of place, appearing to be in search of something or somebody. As we got closer, his attention zoomed right on us. I didn't recognize him at all, but he immediately seemed to know who we were.

He looked at my brother first and said, "Excuse me, but are you by any chance Vivien's sons?"

My brother quickly replied, "Yes, we are, and who are you?"

The man put out his hand and answered, "You might not recognize me, but I am your father's best friend from Chicago."

He told us his name and continued, "I know you guys were too little to remember me, but if you two would like to meet your father, he is right outside waiting for you."

We looked through the glass doors to the parking lot where this man was pointing. Our father was in the black Lincoln less than twenty-five yards from us. He went on to say that it was completely up to us and that our father would understand if we chose not to see him.

My brother and I looked at each other, completely dumbfounded.

"So, what do you think? Should we?" my brother asked.

I replied that we should walk some more and think about it. He agreed. Our father's friend told us to take all the time we needed and assured us they would be right outside, waiting.

It was beyond my ability to handle how fast our lives were being upended and in such a short amount of time. Just a few months earlier, I was talking to Mom in my kitchen about the possibility of meeting my real father someday, and now here he was, waiting outside her funeral service.

It didn't take long before my brother and I headed back to the entrance with a decision. We were ready to take on this huge moment and meet our father, who we had not seen for thirteen years. As we walked out the glass doors toward his black rental car, all I could think about was, *What does this man look like?*

All I could visualize was black sideburns and greased-back hair. My brother had a stronger memory of him, which became apparent when he immediately bolted toward our father the moment he saw him. They almost butted heads trying to get their arms around each other, and the embrace was very emotional. I stood watching them but was not connecting with this like my brother. I moved in to get my hug and could tell by the intense squeeze dad gave me that this was a big deal for him.

The emotions and all the catching up would have to be put on hold as our father explained that nobody knew he was in town, and it was important that we kept it that way. We made plans to meet at the local Bennigan's later that day as everybody went their separate ways.

I have just three words to describe the meeting that

took place with our father that July afternoon: "Mom was right!"

One of the first questions out of this man's mouth was, "Why haven't you two responded back to me? After all the years of Christmas gifts and birthday gifts that I have sent you, you can't even send me a thank-you?"

It sounded insane to us, and he probably gathered that from the looks on our faces.

He went on to give us the play-by-play on what happened that first Saturday he came to pick us up. The moving trucks were parked in front of the house, and nobody would tell him anything. He had gone over to Danna's house to get some information, but she would not tell him anything.

Our reunion quickly turned into a one-sided conversation all about him and how our disappearance had affected him. Don't get me wrong, I have always understood that he was just as much a victim in this as we were. However, at that moment, on the day of our mother's funeral, I felt strongly that he should have been far more worried about us and how we were holding up than insisting we knew how unfair this was to him.

We did our best to explain that we knew nothing about any gifts sent from him and certainly did not receive any. That just made him more upset, and it didn't seem to matter what we said, the conversation continued to be about him. At one point, the conversation did actually become about us, but sadly it was just him pointing out how ridiculous he thought we both looked. My brother's teased up Duran Duran hairstyle, complete with a *Miami Vice* jacket and neck bandanna along with my "40 pounds of Bon Jovi curl" and multicolored rubber bracelets, did not set well with him at all. In fact, at one point he had the audacity to ask my brother if he was gay.

I sat there as Mom's soft voice ran through my head with those words, "I just don't want you to get your hopes up, Bradley Mark. I wouldn't want you to be disappointed." And fortunately, because of her loving advice, I was not. The only thing I really was, was relieved. Relieved that I would never have to wonder what I might have been missing had I never reunited with this man. I knew at that very moment I had missed out on nothing.

14

YOUNG, WILD, AND FREE

Before the summer of '86 ended, my brother and I made some immediate decisions that would start out our new young lives without Mom in a positive direction. We did go back to Chicago for a week to visit our father and his third wife. We discovered we had a half sister from his second marriage, and we got a chance to meet some of our family members from his side. All in all, it was something we probably needed to do, and it felt good to know there was family that had always thought of us and were concerned for our well-being. I came back assured that I would have no interest in establishing any kind of relationship with my father, though my brother very much did. He always felt more connected to this man than did I, and that was how it would play out for many years.

At the turn of 1987, my brother, now twenty-two, would make his move to LA to pursue a career as a musician/bass player. I was now twenty, and all I wanted more than anything else was to let all the pain of the past go and just live. I wanted to live in the moment of being in my twenties in the eighties! And do it with no regrets or concern over what anybody thought. There was a great song in the eighties by the group Triumph called *Magic Power* that best describes my heart during that time.

I'm young now, I'm wild now, and I want to be free,
Got the magic power of the music in me.

I refused to be sad, and I knew Mom wanted nothing more than for me to celebrate the spirit she had given to me, to let go and just absorb the music, the friends, and all that this rocking decade had for me!

The year also brought the most successful album Bon Jovi would ever release. *Slippery When Wet* made the band a household name, and I was by far one of Jon Bon Jovi's biggest fans. I had the hair, I loved the music, and whenever I was decked out in my '80s wardrobe, some even thought I was him—so much so that I adopted the nickname "Brad Jovi!" I actually convinced a group of young ladies at our table one night at the club that I was him. I told them I was between shows and was only in town for one night. I had the help of my buddies to go along, and before we knew it, I was signing autographs left and right. It got completely out of control to the point that we finally had to tell everybody my limo was waiting, and I had to catch a plane.

By the time the '90s came around, I had experienced the pain of a broken heart on more than one occasion and decided that love was not a game I wanted to play. I had a real struggle trusting women at that point in my life and was convinced that nothing lasted forever anyway, so why try? My perspective was certainly a direct result of being raised through divorce. I was convinced that marriages did not last and that divorce was inevitable. Deep down, I believed everybody cheated, and no one in a relationship was ever totally honest. And at the core of all this dysfunctional thinking was pain over my sweet, loving mother, who made me a promise that she would never leave, but most certainly did. The only woman I ever truly loved broke my heart, and I had a really hard time with that. So, when it came to having a chance at a real committed relationship, I was lost. I was clearly damaged, and the worst part was that I didn't even know it. I was determined to have as much fun as I possibly could and never look back. Life was just one big party, and I was everybody's favorite host.

By then, I had transitioned from head chef in the kitchen to the position I had always wanted. The owners of the Green Parrot had opened a second location that happened to be in the old Picasso building and offered me the opportunity to become a bartender and DJ for them at the brand new Green Parrot West. I must say, I took to it like a duck to water and never looked back. The movie *Cocktail* had just been released, and it seemed everybody wanted to be a bartender. I had found my passion. That little boy from Chicago peeking down the hall to witness Mom's house parties was now hosting his own and getting paid for it. I committed to this new career change full force, and that is when it started to become more than just a job. It was my whole life. Working all night and sleeping all day became the normal schedule. Nightclubs closed at 3 a.m., and if there was an after-hours party, which there often was, I wasn't getting home until the break of dawn.

What started out as recreational fun and a new lease on life after Mom's death soon became a way of living. Though I had always been a hard worker, I was all consumed by the nightlife.

By 1995, and nine years after Mom's passing, I was spinning out of control. The nightclub hours were brutal enough without the after-hour parties and alcohol. But, with them, I never stood a chance. I worked all night and slept all day—night after night, week after week. And my days off were spent binging with lots of vodka, too much cocaine, and very little sleep until it was time to go back to work, and then the cycle repeated all over again.

I made tons of money but never had any. Between my salary and tips, I was clearing over $2,000 a week and still couldn't keep my rent paid on time. It was clear that something needed to change before my life simply imploded.

Finally, in the fall of 1997, I had reached the point of no return and knew down deep in my heart that it was time. Time to let it all go. No more booze, no more drugs, and no more waking up with the guilt and embarrassment of how my life had turned out. I was just "sick and tired of being sick and tired," and I had now broken Mom's heart. She would have never wanted this for me, and I knew if she were there, she would have never let it continue.

Once I realized how sad I knew she must be, continuing this way was not an option. What started in the '80s as a great time of recreational spirit and beer bong parties had descended into a self-destructive way of escaping from all the years of pain. I decided to stop walking this dark path I was on, and the plan I made was one I would share with nobody.

My brother was to get married on Christmas Eve that year, and I was going to be his best man, so I knew trying to sober up then would just set me up for failure. After all, it was a celebration, and alcoholics are always looking for an excuse. And following that meaningful event would be one of the biggest excuses ever to get smashed: New Year's Eve. So, I decided that I would finally put an end to "Brad Jovi" the party boy after one last hoorah to bring in the new year. And, most importantly, to bring in a brand new me.

I spared no expense in making my last New Year's Eve as the party host as big as I could: from the traditional rented limousine full of friends to all the necessary party favors. I would go out on the town for great live music, nonstop dancing and celebration, with all those who had partied alongside me for years. This one, however, felt different—more special than all the others put together for one reason more than any. It was my last, and I knew it. After this night, my life was going to change, and I knew there would be no turning back. What I couldn't have known, however, was how this newfound sobriety would be received. What would all those who had known me as the life of the party and indulged right alongside me for years think?

The night rolled into the next day for me, and by the time it was all over and the last drop of booze was gone, it was noon on New Year's Day 1998. I woke the limo driver up from the couch and asked that he take me home. As I walked up the stairs to my apartment, I looked toward the ground-level apartment where my neighbor's children were playing by their front door. I would see these two boys often, and they would always greet me with a smile, but this time it was different. They slowly looked up at me when I said hello, and did not respond. They just looked at me with blank faces and turned back to what they were doing. It was as if they knew I had been out all night partying and were extremely disappointed in me. It felt very strange and something that has always stuck with me.

I walked back to my bedroom and into my bathroom and just stared into the mirror, looking at a man I no longer recognized, a man who looked like he hadn't slept for a week, and a man who knew the madness was finally over. A man who was once just a little boy from Chicago. A boy who was swept up in a web of mafia crime, witness protection, and permanent relocation. An innocent victim of circumstance who was allowed no choice in how it would all play out. And now this once innocent boy stood broken, addicted, lost and all alone. I paused as my eyes filled with tears, and I said to that man in the mirror, "Bradley, it's over. It's finally all over. It's time to take your life back."

I stepped from the mirror and, with one last look at my burned-out face, mumbled, "Never again. Never, never again."

EPILOGUE

A proud Dad (me) hanging out with his amazing
kids on graduation day.

There is no doubt the single best decision I made in
my life was saying goodbye to my addiction to
drugs and alcohol, and finally exiting my path of self-

destruction. This newfound clarity brought me to realize how truly amazing life actually was.

Just over a year into sobriety, I was blessed with my first child: a beautiful little six-pound four-ounce baby girl named Taylor Maye'lee. And just three short years later came a beautiful son, Tanner Bradley. With fatherhood my new focus, there seemed to be no turning back. I was committed to a new life with a new family and a chance to create a better scenario for my children than the one that was created for me.

Though my marriage to their mother came to an end when the kids were still very young, it wouldn't be long before another blessing would come my way. In 2011, I met the absolute love of my life, and four years later, Johnna Marshalle Morrow became my wife. She brought to me everything I had ever been missing: true love, true commitment, and a true best friend. But, above all, she allowed me to realize that the deep void inside me could only be filled with one thing. And that one thing was God. Not booze or drugs, not money or relationships. I had spent my whole life convinced it was all about me only to find out that nothing could have been further from the truth. The fact is, it was never about me. Never once. It has always and forever been about Him.

The introduction to this Truth in my life changed everything—the way I saw my kids, my finances, and even the way I saw myself from the outside looking in. I was no longer just a victim of my circumstance. I was never just a "stepson to the mob."

I am now twenty-four years clean and sober, and those beautiful children of mine are all grown up—attending college and blazing their own exciting trail. My amazing wife and I are now living the ultimate dream. We set a plan five years ago to finally start a new life in the very place Mom had always wanted to live: Florida! And now that dream has come true in a beautiful city on South Florida's Atlantic coast called Hobe Sound, just minutes from the beach, where the palm trees sway, and the sunshine never ends. There's no doubt she is looking down from Heaven with that amazing smile, boasting, "Bradley Mark, I am so proud of you, and I always knew you would live out our dream!"

When we began this journey together, I emphasized how instrumental our decisions are in determining the outcome of our lives. Every decision we make has a consequence. No matter how much disfunction we may have been dealt as a child, we all eventually get to choose how we handle the results. We all get a chance to make our own decisions on the direction of our lives. When I was a small boy, my direction was clearly decided for me based on a slew of bad decisions made by adults. As a teenager, I began making my own share of bad choices, and my direction began to falter. And after Mom's death, my decision to mask the pain eventually led to the kinds of choices that could have killed me. But they didn't. And it's simply because it was not my time to go. God had a different plan for me, and it was far better than the one I had made for myself.

If there is anything I have learned about my life and about this journey I have shared, it is that no matter how bad things get, you're just one good decision away from turning it all around.

Then there is the question of forgiveness. It is something that can never be given by anyone who refuses to let go—to let go of hate and, most importantly, to let go of pain caused by another. If we can't do this, then we simply can't move on. I was quick to forgive my mother for all the mistakes that she made. Regardless of the pain they might have caused me, I knew her decisions came from a place of love and devotion for her two boys. With Al, it was not so easy. In fact, it seemed like an impossibility. After all, this was all his fault. He was never who he said he really was—nothing more than a common criminal.

Then, one day, it hit me. I don't forgive Al for his sake. I forgive him for mine. In order for God to have opened the door for me to finally tell my story, I had to fulfill His wish, to forgive all who have failed me. And that meant everyone.

And so I have. And, in doing so, it brought me the closure that I so desperately needed. It brought me freedom from the guilt and shame that I had felt for many years. And it ultimately gave me the opportunity to share my journey. And, for that, I am beyond grateful. Thank you for taking the time to open this book and for allowing me to tell the story of a true hero, one for which there is no replacement: my mom.

Finally home! With our toes in the sand and sunshine on our shoulders, there is no doubt, dreams do come true!

www.ingramcontent.com/pod-product-compliance
Lightning Source LLC
Chambersburg PA
CBHW070125030426

42335CB00016B/2276